In an ancient blood feud that will never die,
it's time to choose a side . . .

Think you know Robert Pattinson?
One of the most famous young actors on the planet,
his name and face are everywhere. But this comprehensive biography
takes you closer than ever before. Starting from the very beginning,
Bonded by Blood recounts Pattinson's London childhood, his early
forays into amateur dramatics, and his teenage roles before
Twilight made him a global phenomenon.

Detailing Robert's life-changing experiences working on
The Twilight Saga – his pivotal first audition, his relationships with
his co-stars, and gossip from the *Eclipse* shoot – this book also explores
the haunting world of Stephenie Meyer's novels, how Edward Cullen
was brought from dream to screen, and exactly why
Team Edward is the right choice for you.

Featuring many stunning full-colour photographs of Robert,
Bonded by Blood reveals how he copes with constant media scrutiny,
the truth about his relationship with Kristen Stewart, the controversy
surrounding *Remember Me,* and up-to-date information on future films,
including *Eclipse* and *Breaking Dawn.* If you're keen to join the Cullen
coven, everything you could possibly want to know – and more – is here.

Garrett Baldwin is an alum of the Medill School of Journalism
at Northwestern University and has written for a variety of political
publications in Washington DC, where he resides. He is currently
earning his Masters Degree in international economic and
energy security at Johns Hopkins University.

Bonded by Blood

Robert Pattinson Biography

Garrett Baldwin

Plexus, London

For John Tansor and William Tinsley

British Library Cataloguing in Publication Data
A catalogue record for this book is available from the British Library.

ISBN-10: 0-85965-461-3
ISBN-13: 978-0-85965-461-6

Cover photograph by Rune Hellestad/Corbis/Armando Gallo/Retna Ltd./Corbis
Book and cover design by Coco Wake-Porter
Printed in Great Britain by Cromwell Press Group

Contents

Introduction 7

1. Barnes Beginnings 9

2. Advice from Dad 15

3. Just Like Jack 23

4. A Magical Ride 29

5. Summertime in London 35

6. Indie Peaks and Valleys 43

7. Chicago Cullen 51

8. The Search for Edward Cullen 59

9. Becoming Edward Cullen 69

10. Pattinson on Tour 80

11. Life Without Edward 86

12. The Case for Team Edward 93

13. Star-crossed Crossroads 98

14. Today's Actor, Tomorrow's Rock Star 105

15. The Year of Robert Pattinson 111

Acknowledgments

The author would like to thank the Weinig family, Sandra Wake and the editorial team at Plexus: Tom Branton, Laura Coulman and Coco Wake-Porter for this opportunity and their remarkable work, and the good men at ESPN, Matthew Berry and Nate Ravitz, for their world-class advice on American pop culture.

Robert Pattinson has given many interviews to newspapers, magazines, television shows and websites, and these have proved invaluable in chronicling his life and career. The author and editors would like to give special thanks to *The Sunday Times, Daily Express, Daily Mail, Daily Mirror, Sunday Mirror, Daily Star, Oregon Herald, Los Angeles Times, The Star-Ledger, The Independent, The New York Post, The Chicago Sun-Times, Star Magazine, Seattle Post-Intelligencer, The New York Times, The Times, Interview Magazine, Metro News, Teen Vogue, The Sun, The Telegraph, The Daily Mirror, Teen Magazine, Vanity Fair, The Guardian, E! Online, Details Magazine, Us Weekly, Fangoria, People, Life & Style, Empire, Gone with the Twins, Entertainment Weekly, GQ Magazine, Explore Magazine, Rolling Stone, Chicago Tribune, Vogue, Clevver Tv, The Hollywood Reporter, TMZ,* radiofree.com, efilmcritic.com, about.com, ivillage.com, buddytv. com, twilightersanonymous.com, hollyscoop.com, *glamourmagazine.co.uk,* buzzingtwilight.com, canmag.com, , reelzchannel.com, acedmagazine.com, mtv.com, metronews.ca, examiner.com, twilightcartel.com, petitiononline.com, thepetitionsite.com, twilightmoms.com, seventeen.com, movies.msn.com, ontheflix.com, newmoonmovie.org, eclipsemovie.com, stepheniemeyer.com, twilightthemovie.com, lionandlamblove.org, eclipsemovie.org, radaronline.com, twilighters.org, thedeadbolt.com, robert-pattinson.co.uk, robertpattinsononline.com, robertpattinsonau.com, robertpattinson.org, robert.pattinson.free.fr, robert-pattinson.net, robert-pattinson.co.uk, mirror. co.uk, robsessedpattinson.com, pattinsonladies.blogspot.com, TheCelebrityCafe.com, okmagazine. com, icould.com, thinkingofrob.com, moviesonline.com, contactmusic.com, agirlsworld.com, robertpattinsonunlimited.com, collider.com, telegraph.co.uk, thesun.co.uk, totalscifionline.com, www.robertpattinsonau.com, robert-p-daily.com, hangbag.com, movietome.com, sugarslam.com, dailymotion.com, ugo.com, nydailynews.com, showbizspy.com, twifans.com, reelzchannel.com.

The following books were used in research: *New Moon, Twilight, Eclipse, Breaking Dawn* by Stephenie Meyer, *Twilight: The Complete Illustrated Movie Companion, New Moon: The Complete Illustrated Movie Companion* by Mark Cotta Vaz, *The Robert Pattinson Album* by Paul Stenning, *Robert Pattinson: The Unauthorized Biography* by Virginia Blackburn. Thanks are also due to the film distributors: Summit Entertainment, Dimension Films, Twentieth Century-Fox Film Corporation, Karz Entertainment; the following television shows, films and stations: *Late Night with Jimmy Fallon, Jimmy Kimmel Live!, CBS and its affiliates, The Ellen DeGeneres Show, E! Entertainment, MTV Networks, NBC and its affiliates, ABC and its affiliates, Robsessed, BBC News, Channel 4, Access Hollywood, Moviefone's Unscripted, The Late Show with David Letterman, Univision Foro, IFC.*

We would like to thank the following for supplying photographs: Corbis/Peter Andrews; Tower House School Photograph/Evening Standard; Bliss Magazine; Barnes Theatre Company; Getty Images/Stringer/Dave Hogan; Getty Images/WireImage/Ferdaus Shamin; Rex Features/ Everett Collection/Regent; Getty Images/WireImage/Jim Spellman; Getty Images/WireImage/ Kevin Mazur/TCA 2009; Getty Images/Franco Origlia; Getty Images/Franco Origlia; Contour by Getty Images/Jeff Riedel; Contour by Getty Images/Jeff Riedel; Corbis/People Avenue/Stephane Cardinale; Getty Images/Vittorio Zunino Celotto; Getty Images/WireImage/Alexandra Wyman; Getty Images/WireImage/Kevin Mazur; Getty Images/WireImage/George Pimentel; Getty Images/ WireImage/Dominique Charriau; Getty Images/WireImage/Fotonoticias; Rex Features/Theo Kingma; Rex Features/Everett Collection; Rex Features/Charles Sykes; Rex Features/Europress Photo Agency; Getty Images/WireImage/Jon Furniss; Corbis/Retna Ltd/Armando Gallo.

Every effort has been made to acknowledge and trace copyright holders and to contact original sources, and we apologize for any unintentional errors which will be corrected in future editions of this book.

Introduction

'I remember when I was younger I used to write in my diary:
I want my luck to be spread. Never give me anything too lucky all at once.
I'll take a little luck now and then, but spread it for seventy years. Now that all
of this is happening, I'm sure the rest of my life will be ruined.'
– Robert Pattinson

At twenty-four years old, Robert Pattinson has experienced a rare Hollywood ascendancy that has abruptly catapulted him to the heights of international acclaim. A remarkably dashing young man known as much for his acting skills as his tousled hair and distinctive jaw line, Rob has established himself as one of film's brightest stars, a talent expected to shine for years to come.

To describe his rise as meteoric would be an understatement, as in fewer than five years he has advanced from a minor, secondary role in the *Harry Potter* franchise to being the overexposed face of the international phenomenon that is Stephenie Meyer's *Twilight* series. Defined by a disarming charm and self-deprecating personality, Robert fires the blazing hearts of millions whenever he appears on-screen as the icy romantic vampire Edward Cullen.

The youngest child of a middle-class family from London, Robert experienced a pleasant childhood that provided no hint of future stardom. But from an early age, it was evident to his mentors and those around him that he possessed a number of unique qualities that made him stand out from his classmates. A talented musician who began learning guitar and piano before his fifth birthday, Rob can truly be deemed an artist, one whose innate creativity remains very much in evidence away from films sets.

He rose quickly through the ranks of the Barnes Theater Group and London acting community, his first break coming after he was spotted by a talent agent during one of his amateur productions. But after his first taste of international acclaim in *Harry Potter and the Goblet of Fire*, the Londoner mysteriously retreated to smaller, character-driven films that barely attracted the attention of audiences or critics. Having no formal training in acting, Robert abandoned scripts reserved for teen heartthrobs and sought to educate himself in how to perform. His unusual path to international acclaim led him to an awkward, intimate audition with Kristen Stewart on the bed of *Twilight* director Catherine Hardwicke, and continues to this day with the highly anticipated release of the series' third film, *Eclipse*.

Standing outside the London premiere of his film *Remember Me* in March 2010, Robert stuttered in explaining his precipitous rise to stardom. 'I remember I did a *Harry Potter* film premiere here like four or five years ago, and this all happened. And then the next day I was walking through here again going to auditions and stuff and it didn't make any difference. And now,' he said, pausing while the screams of hundreds of women echoed his name, 'I don't know what happened. I just sort of fell on a runaway train.'

As fans call his name again on the red carpet this June, gushing over his stunning looks and dreaming of their own intimate moment in the meadow with the brooding Edward Cullen, Robert himself is forever bound by *Eclipse*'s tragic love triangle, which has divided a legion of fans between his Team Edward and Taylor Lautner's Team Jacob. The heart-wrenching choice that Bella Swan must make between her two loves in the story's climax has spawned international debate about which actor's character can fulfill her hopes of eternal love. More so, it has heightened the acclaim surrounding both Pattinson and Lautner, whose very different lives conjoin for the on-screen adaptation of Stephenie Meyer's third novel.

Each actor has his own story. Each has experienced the trials and tribulations, the peaks and valleys, the rejections and the praise of a Hollywood existence. Rob Pattinson's is a life of blithe independence; he is a talented young man in search of purpose, dabbling in art for art's sake. Disconnected from the idea of celebrity, he's a rare personality who takes immense joy in performing on screen, but never in front of a paparazzo's camera. His search for complex roles, a testament to his hero Jack Nicholson, is a reminder of why we go to the movies in the first place: to watch artists perform and to experience the emotions they bring to life in every scene.

Robert Pattinson is clearly a superstar, a remarkably talented, yet undeniably individual actor who commits his emotional range and thespian talent to any script he finds endearing. The coming years will prove to be evermore successful for Robert, whether it be due to his role in the blockbuster *Eclipse* or a tiny independent movie that requires his appearance in only a few frames. Robert continually seeks a plethora of challenging roles that force him to grow and evolve as an actor and as a person, and, with time, will offer him the chance to become not just Hollywood's most in-demand actor, but one of its most respected.

1
Barnes Beginnings

'I was never one of those kids at three years old, on stage dancing.'
– Robert Pattinson

Robert Thomas Pattinson was born in a private clinic near London on Tuesday, 13 May 1986. The only son of Richard and Clare Pattinson, he was the couple's youngest of three children. Five years prior, Robert's parents had welcomed their first daughter, Victoria, followed by their second, Elizabeth, who was born in 1983. The arrival of the blonde-locked Robert delivered a great deal of joy to his family. His older sisters, then three and five years of age, would now have an animated doll to dress up and play with, and his father soon had an ally in what had until that point been a female-dominated household. Robert was a jubilant child with an intrinsic shyness and independent curiosity that would later distinguish his adult personality. Given his traditional upbringing, and the fact that he walked a somewhat meandering path between his acting and musical passions, no one could have predicted his meteoric rise to celebrity 'it-ism'.

The road to Hollywood stardom today is paved in the nepotistic networks of established celebrity royalty, providing very few opportunities for newcomers. Although his mother's position as a scout for a leading modeling agency would later present the teenage Robert with modeling opportunities, 'Patty', as he was known, did not grow up on film sets or break into Hollywood the way so many younger actors of his generation have, edging through the doors of stardom at a young age via their family's personal or professional connections. 'I wasn't really an actor as a kid,' Robert said, repeatedly stating that his path to the cover of seemingly every gossip magazine didn't start with a preternatural love of performing. 'I was never one of those kids at three years old, on stage dancing.' Thousands of miles and an ocean away from the lights and glamour of Los Angeles, the Pattinsons were a well-heeled, middle-class family making ends meet through the entrepreneurial spirit of both parents.

'My father left school – I think he will probably tell me off on this – I think he was fifteen, and doesn't really have that many formal qualifications,' Victoria Pattinson said. 'And my mother also left school when she was quite young, and she trained to be a dress designer. So quite a sort of vocational skill, and she worked in the fashion business before she had kids. My father ended up working in the car business.' Robert Pattinson has said on more than one occasion that their father lived in the United States at some point in the 1970s, working as a taxi driver. He later moved to London where he began importing and selling classic cars in the 1980s. While Richard's advice and professional success would later become guiding influences along his son's boulevard to the big screen, Robert has joked that he never sought to venture into his father's profession, and would certainly think twice about becoming one of Richard's customers.

'My dad told me a lot of stories,' Robert said with a laugh. 'I would never buy a car from him.' Originally from Yorkshire, Richard Pattinson met his wife, Clare, in a quaint pub in Richmond, Surrey through a mutual friend. Clare was the youngest of three daughters and grew up near Richmond Hill, not far from the fortuitous pub where she first encountered her future husband. They would soon marry when Clare was twenty-six and Richard thirty-five. Richard's successful vintage-car business afforded the family some comfort and enabled them to settle in the pleasant confines of Barnes, an affluent West London suburb that traces the Thames River. The Pattinson family resided in a £1-million, five-bedroom Victorian semi, just a short train ride from Central London. Originally part of Surrey, Barnes village dates back to the 11th century and currently hosts some of the oldest houses in London, with one road, The Terrace, featuring residences that were built in the 1720s and attract bids of several million pounds.

Barnes offered the perfect setting for a contented childhood, providing numerous influences in Robert's early development and a bounty of resources for young actors and musicians. Barnes is home to many of England's most renowned athletes, broadcasters, politicians and actors. Despite its proximity to London, certain areas of Barnes retain the sleepy feel of the countryside, most notably Barnes Pond, which hosts several open-air and covered markets each month. With its historical music connections, Barnes is perhaps most famous as the home of Olympic Studios, which relocated from downtown London in 1966 after it was purchased by moguls Cliff Adams and Keith Grant. Over the past few decades, the recording studios on Church Road have hosted many of rock and pop's greatest legends, most notably the Beatles and the Rolling Stones, the latter of whom recorded six LPs at the location. Other musicians who have recorded there include Ella Fitzgerald, Jimi Hendrix, the Verve, Pink Floyd, Coldplay, Queen, Led Zeppelin, Eric Clapton, U2, the Arctic Monkeys, David Bowie, and the Who.

Not far from the studios, at the end of Lonsdale Road, the Bull's Head pub is known as one of the first and most important jazz venues in Britain, opened not long after World War Two. Barnes is also famous for being the site of rock musician Marc Bolan's fatal car crash on Queen's Ride in 1977. The scene of the accident now hosts Bolan's Rock Shrine, a memorial that receives recurrent visits from fans. In 2002, fans installed a bronze bust of the musician to mark the twenty-fifth anniversary of his death.

But most significantly, Barnes remains highly regarded for its thespian roots, with a large, established acting community. The Old Sorting Office arts center, adjacent to Barnes Pond, is regarded as one of London's most esteemed venues for art and fringe theater, hosting several popular theater productions each year. Well-established actors and actresses (aside from the now world-famous Robert Pattinson) to have performed at the venue include Stephanie Cole, Patricia Hodge, Timothy West, and Julian Glover. The culture and the wealth surrounding him in Barnes failed to distract Robert during his formative years. Even now, despite his ever-increasing fame, worldwide appeal, and a luxurious Los Angeles apartment, Pattinson still returns home regularly to disengage from the outside world in a celebrity poster-clad room at his parents' house, telling reporters, 'I would never move from this city, I adore London.'

The youngest of three children, Robert was naturally the victim of teasing and girlish torment by his older sisters. It is well known that siblings Victoria and Lizzy dressed him up like a girl and introduced him to their family and friends as 'Claudia' until he reached the age of twelve. It is this early playful teasing and role-play that seemed to have provided the groundwork for Robert's disarming charm and humility, and later for his loving relationship with his older sisters.

Despite the closeness of his family life, Rob has always described himself as something of a loner, his present unease in the public eye apparently rooted in his childhood shyness. While his first school, Tower Preparatory, attempted to instill the virtues of gentlemanly behavior and social skills, Robert, for the most part, preferred solitude and the opportunity to explore his own imagination. 'I didn't have very many toys [growing up], I used to just to play with a pack of cards all the time,' Robert laughed.

'I'd pretend the cards were other things. I liked any toy that didn't involve playing with other children.' He would later admit that he didn't even like it when strangers made eye contact, saying that he'd freak out on the bus if anyone stared at him. 'I'm a very paranoid person. I've spent my whole life feeling like everyone's looking at me, ever since I was a little kid. And then when people come up to me it's like, "*Proof!* See they were looking at me."'

While Robert is vocal about his desire for privacy concerning his past and present life, and remains relatively close-lipped about his childhood, the same cannot always be said of certain of his relatives. In April 2009 *Life & Style* magazine interviewed his aunt Diana Nutley and ran pictures of Robert at a very young age. Those pictures accompanied his aunt's short quip about a young Robert 'hamming it up at family gatherings'. 'I remember we had a party in the garden one July,' Nutley told *Life & Style*. 'We had a wonderful game to see how many doughnuts we could eat without licking our lips. It's impossible – Rob was covered in jam.' Another aunt, Monica Weller, spoke a little later to another magazine that had run a picture of young Robert riding a tricycle. 'I could say there were signs when he was growing up he was going to be a heartbreaker,' Weller said.

Robert's reaction in the press to his aunts' revelations hinted at his discomfort with such media attention. Featuring a mildly chubby blonde with a resplendent smile, the pictures revealed an ordinary, mischievous child, one whose days were spent in the joys of doughnuts and bike rides rather than the burdensome lifestyle of a child actor. Shortly after these pictures were published, Robert – then twenty-three, established in Hollywood, and lusted after all around the world – appeared somewhat rattled by their release. 'Really?' he asked when a tabloid reporter sought comment. 'It's just so embarrassing.' He would, in the same breath, go on to suggest that publication of his child photographs should be illegal, although his breezy deliverance implied his comment was little more than a joke, and further evidence of his desire to remove himself from the ever-increasing spotlight focused upon his life.

Aside from jam-covered shirts, little suggests that Robert was an unruly child, which was fortunate for him given that his secondary school maintained strict rudimentary standards. Robert had been playing the piano since he was 'three or four years old' and the guitar from the age of five, and, by this time, he had learned basic skills from his parents and sisters. His soon-to-be-discovered passion for acting, however, would be driven by an ongoing love-hate relationship with his first-class education and take-home studies. Tower House Preparatory, his first school, is an independent academy in East Sheen for young boys aged four to thirteen. According to the school's curriculum, Tower House teaches students both in groups and individually, enabling each child to discover and cultivate their own talents and educational skills. At the time, it appeared that music would provide the talented young Londoner's ultimate direction.

Robert's thespian talents were nurtured by the school's pro-acting curriculum. The school offered Robert half-hour speech and drama lessons during the day, but he seems to have developed amnesia in regard to his early acting experiences. ('I never did acting at school. I was quite shy throughout my life,' Robert said.) But by the age of six Robert was already performing in amateur productions. One of his teachers had written a play entitled *Spell for a Rhyme*, in which Robert assumed his first part, that of the mystical King of Hearts (a character that would certainly please a boy fascinated by his deck of cards).

But while Robert began to excel in acting and public speaking, he was showing a growing disinterest in academia. He was acknowledged in a 1998 school newsletter as the 'runaway winner of last term's Form Three untidy desk award', and there was some concern growing about Robert's barefaced refusal to do homework and keep up with his studies. Although he was evidently a bright young man, capable of paying attention and following the curriculum, it was beginning to appear that his school work simply wasn't of interest or importance to him. Due to this academic apathy, his grades naturally suffered. 'School reports were always pretty bad – I never ever did my homework,' Robert said. 'I always turned up for lessons as I liked my teachers, but my report said I didn't try very hard.'

Still, Robert's parents did not overreact to his poor academic performance, recognizing that he was inspired in other areas such as music and acting. As Caroline Booth, school secretary at Tower House, told the *London Evening Standard*, 'Robert wasn't a particularly academic child but he always loved drama. He was an absolutely lovely boy, everyone adored him. We have lots of lovely boys here, but he was something special.'

As he progressed through school, he would soon begin to learn the importance of hard work and savings through his daily paper route, from which he earned £10 to £15 each week. As it was clear that paper delivery was not his life's ambition, he began to seek any rationale for pursuing a particular field or occupation. At the time, there was only one central requirement for any future profession. 'I wanted to do something which didn't involve doing homework,' Robert said. 'That was the one thing I was clear about when I was a kid. I knew I didn't want to do any more. I wanted to do something that involved being told what to do as little as possible.'

While it may appear that acting requires a great deal of direction (read: people telling him what to do), Robert would later focus on the freedom of interpretation and imagination that the profession offered. Perhaps it was not the idea of being told what to do that really bothered the young Robert, but rather being told how to think.

Despite an outwardly poor memory of his early acting days, it was evident that Robert had developed an enthusiasm for and degree of comfort on the stage while at Tower House. This experience would steer him towards roles that shared superficial similarities with the *Twilight* series. After his part in *Spell for a Rhyme*, he appeared in his school's adaptation of *Lord of the Flies*, playing the role of Robert.

The play was based on the book of the same title, written by William Golding and published in the first few first years of the Cold War. In the story, a plane crash leaves only young British schoolchildren as survivors on a deserted island. The boys – all thirteen years old or younger – must now adapt and learn to coexist. The story portrays their descent into savagery as the well-educated children regress to a primitive state and divide into rival camps who battle each other for survival; opposing clans much like the Quileute tribe and Cullen family in Stephenie Meyer's *Twilight Saga*, or indeed, the dedicated *Twilight* fans who would become members of either Taylor Lautner's Team Jacob or Robert Pattinson's Team Edward.

2

Advice from Dad

'I started doing plays when I was about fifteen or sixteen. I only did it because my dad saw a bunch of pretty girls in a restaurant and he asked them where they came from and they said drama group. He said, "Son, that is where you need to go."'
– Robert Pattinson

Perhaps Robert wasn't always meant to be the Pattinson family's great success story. After all, there were two sisters who came before him, both with academic ambition and the drive to succeed. Richard and Clare Pattinson recognized early on that their children had unique talents, each requiring different levels of attention and encouragement. Elizabeth, three years older and no longer dressing Robert up as 'Claudia', had become a beautiful, five-foot-eight blonde by her mid-teens. Slender-framed with green eyes, she too had a growing passion for music, one that steered her toward interpretive dance in her youth. After receiving a Grade Eight in ballet, the alto-voiced Lizzy decided she would enter the music business. She didn't benefit from any direct connections to producers or talent scouts. Instead she relied on raw talent and note-perfect vocals. Lizzy's path to musical success started in the various clubs and pubs around Barnes village – including the Sun Inn – and other hotspots in Central London. A talent scout at EMI Records eventually spotted Lizzy, then only seventeen, during one of her amateur performances, and invited her to become a member of the internationally acclaimed dance band Aurora. Within months, the band released two tracks – 'Dreaming' and 'The Day It Rained Forever' – both of which reached the UK Top Thirty. Aurora put on concerts throughout Britain, Europe, and North America, with the size of their live audiences reaching more than 100,000 people. After teaming up with house music producers Milk & Sugar, Lizzy reached Number One on the Billboard Dance Chart in the US with the hit track 'Let the Sunshine In' (the song reached Number 16 in the UK). She would also collaborate on songs featured in *Twilight*, adding background vocals, most notably on the Carter Burwell song 'Who Are They'. (This song can be heard when Bella first sees Edward Cullen enter the cafeteria.) Lizzy continues to produce and release music online to her growing fan base. Her most recent single, 'Surrender', was recorded in collaboration with DJ Milo NL and CJ Stone and released by 12 Tone Records. She has also experimented in acting, giving credited performances in recent productions such as Paddy Gormley's *Misanthrope II* and Ian Buckley's *The Return*.

Victoria, the eldest Pattinson child, appears to have inherited her father's business acumen. Yet she too has pursued her creative flair in writing and once considered becoming a journalist. She would later choose to venture into advertising. Victoria's first experience in an ad agency, which came when she was fifteen and had just finished her GCSE exams, was quite unusual. 'I spent the entire week working on cat food brands, which I have no interest in at all, and I don't even like cats either. [That] sort of put me at a slight disadvantage.' She soon took some time away from the marketing industry, and after passing her A-levels, became the first member of the Pattinson family to attend university, where she would find herself indecisive about her career options, an attitude which appears to have become a running theme in the Pattinson household. 'I had absolutely no idea what I wanted to do when I was in school,' Victoria said. 'I knew that I was interested in a broad sense in the communications industry. I was really, really obsessed with magazines and books and newspapers and current affairs.' Victoria was obviously seeking a more traditional corporate track, although the start of her career was far from conventional.

Victoria earned her first job at Sky Television, as the result of an incident that took place while she was out walking her dog one evening. Along the way, Victoria noticed that a neighbor's house had been broken into and a car had been stolen. While the house alarm continued to blare through the Barnes streets, and the police had just arrived, Victoria visited her neighbor's house. After asking if everything was okay at the burgled residence, she began talking to the woman who lived there. Eventually this woman offered her a job and became her first boss at Sky, where Victoria worked on a team launching television stations. 'You really could never plan that kind of interaction,' Victoria said of the chance occurrence. 'It is really an awful thing that happened – that her house was burgled and her car got stolen. That is the most bizarre way I have ever heard of anyone getting a job.'

After spending some time at Sky, she was encouraged to pursue several fellowship opportunities. She was soon awarded a position in the prestigious WPP Group Fellowship Program, during the course of which she spent three years in London and New York. She currently acts as a global business development manager for the advertising mega-conglomerate. 'I really enjoy working with really entrepreneurial people,' she said. 'At some point I would like to run something which may be as a global piece of business or an interesting project of some kind, that is really what I would like to do.'

Richard and Clare Pattinson encouraged all three of their children to explore the full spectrum of what education has to offer. 'They were always quite enthusiastic about encouraging us as kids to try hard in school,' Victoria said. 'And not just in school in a conventional academic sense, and to embrace different passions in the arts or in sport or whatever it was we were interested in.' Though Lizzy and Victoria had shown incredible talent in their respective passions, it had become increasingly evident that Robert possessed something different from his sisters – an extraordinary talent and creativity deserving of advanced cultivation. But Robert has considered another possibility: that of his father's creative aspirations being channeled through the three Pattinson children. 'My dad said to me, "I really am an artistic person." I was shocked as I never saw him as creative. I think me and my sisters are living out that side of him.'

Robert really began to fulfill that dream shortly after leaving Tower House Preparatory for a new school. Although he claims that he was expelled from Tower House ('I got expelled from my school when I was twelve – I was quite bad!') it appears the real reason for the move was simply that Robert's parents wanted to provide him with an environment in which he could expand his extracurricular aspirations. The Harrodian School in Barnes, situated on Lonsdale Road, was closer to the Pattinson family home and, at a cost of £13,500 per year, would guarantee Robert expert tutelage and plentiful opportunities for creative expansion. Renowned for its high academic standards, the Harrodian has produced an intelligent rank of future doctors, lawyers, and bankers. Until now, the only girls chasing Robert had been his sisters. Now, the co-ed preparatory school offered him his first experience of being surrounded by the opposite sex on a near-constant basis. Learning quickly how to befriend and speak with young women, Robert soon found comfort and popularity among his new classmates, admitting that he found his style when he 'moved to a mixed school [. . .] and then I became cool and discovered hair gel'. (Still, Robert does occasionally look back on this time with contradictory views: 'I was a bit of a loner at school, quite antisocial.' He also stated: 'I wasn't with the cool gang or the uncool ones. I was transitional, in between.')

Occasionally he abandoned long-established bad habits where his school career was concerned and actually completed his homework. He soon began taking to the written word, inspired by his favorite English teacher, who encouraged him to write and never criticized his assignments. 'She got me into writing instead of just answering the question,' Robert said. 'I used to hand in homework with twenty pages of nonsense and she'd still mark it. She was a really amazing teacher.' Inspired by this open style of educating, he also began to develop a passion for political debate, even considering becoming a speechwriter for a short period of time, until he recognized that additional academic training would be required for that pursuit. 'I didn't achieve much,' he said, 'but politics was what I wanted to do while I was in school, yeah. I just liked the whole idea of it. I wanted to be involved with politics. That's what my whole plan was. I was going to go to university and then I just thought, "Ah, I can't be bothered to do anything. I don't want to do any more homework!"'

Coincidentally, the hair-gel-equipped Robert's first kiss at the age of twelve soon followed his arrival at a co-ed school environment, although, he confesses, 'I didn't have a girlfriend until I was eighteen.' But while Robert was discovering the foundation of his trademark hairstyle and getting to grips with certain female admirers, modeling agents and photographers were discovering a hidden gem in Barnes. It was only a matter of time before Robert was pushed into modeling, a natural result of his mother's association with a leading European agency. In 2001, Robert's first modeling opportunity came from Miu Miu, a youth-oriented line from the fashion house of Prada. The photographs from the Miu Miu shoot reveal an adolescent with a trademark androgynous look, wearing boxer shorts and flanked by a more experienced blonde model named Lucy Flower. The shoot was reportedly done for the *South China Morning Post*'s weekend magazine. One look at the pictures and it's easy to appreciate how those present on the day don't necessarily recall Robert having an early swagger or allure about him.

'It was kind of one of his first photo shoots, so he wasn't really used to modeling then,' said Lucy Flower, who would later come tenth in the second cycle of *Britain's Next Top Model*. 'And obviously having his mother there probably made him even more nervous, [and] to be modeling with a girl. And to be wearing very little clothes!'

Photographer John-Paul Pietrus, who snapped the pictures, remembers Pattinson as a hip young man with a conflicting look well suited to the shoot. 'Robert had something very mature in his face, but quite teenager in his body, which was exactly what we were going for, because we wanted that teenage vibe,' Pietrus said. 'I thought he was cool right away because he had this sort of class, sort of this sophistication about him which I really liked.'

But Flower remembers a young man who hadn't quite grown out of his shell at the time. 'Robert was such a shy, reserved little boy back then,' she said. 'I never would have thought he had that kind of superstardom ahead of him. Also, I don't believe he was very comfortable with the outfit he had to wear and the fact that he was shirtless. So it's not surprising that he was so quiet and seemed so nervous that day. He was so quiet. He didn't really give that side of his personality that makes you think, "Wow, he's going to be a big star one day."'

Robert's modeling career spanned approximately four years, and he would eventually work for fashion designer Nicole Farhi and the Hackett clothing line, as well as doing fairly regular shoots for spreads in teen magazines. 'I was doing [modeling] at twelve, the youngest person in my agency out of the girls or boys,' he said. 'I was so ridiculously skinny, I looked like a girl, but that was the period where they loved androgynous-looking people.'

Still Robert felt uncomfortable with his look and body. 'I feel like a cartoon character. I look like an idiot – one of my legs is slightly longer than the other. I was such a terrible model. I was really tall but still looked like a six-year-old.' Though he would progress through high school and as a model over the next four years, he would never lose the mysterious, androgynous characteristics that would later define his portrayal of Edward Cullen. Still, his slightly feminine look eventually did give way to puberty and shaving, and dissolved the interest of modeling recruiters and photographers. 'I became too much of a guy, so I never got any more jobs,' Robert explained. 'I had the most unsuccessful modeling career.'

Though Robert still remains unforthcoming about his time at Harrodian, those who knew him back then remember things a bit differently. As he began to develop his now-adored good looks in his mid-teens – he flared his hair while his cheekbones and jaw line became more pronounced – Robert started to establish himself within a number of different crowds. His schoolmate Will Robinson described him as a likable chap during their time at Harrodian. 'Rob had a very, very big grin on his face constantly and was always cheeky in class,' Robinson said. 'Everyone liked him, though. He was a popular kid.'

With his modeling career floundering, Robert began to look for places to explore his creative interests. He would find that artistic outlet when he really began to immerse himself in acting and scene study. He also began to take a more pronounced interest in the girls at Harrodian and started dating, balancing the delicate roles of typical male teen, student, boyfriend and pursuer of extracurricular sports including football, skiing and snowboarding. As his flair for the dramatic became more pronounced, he frequently exaggerated his love life, getting himself worked up in an attempt to explore his emotions, despite the glaringly obvious: he was bemoaning milk that was yet to be spilled. 'I remember when I was a teenager thinking my girlfriend was cheating on me, and going around riling myself up. Pretending to cry. It was totally illegitimate – I actually didn't feel anything. I went to some pub and then went crying all the way home. And I got into my dog's bed. I was crying and holding on to the dog. I woke up in the morning, and the dog was looking at me like, "You're a fake."'

Fake or not, Robert was finally beginning to find true avenues of self expression. Though Harrodian itself produced high-quality drama productions, Robert was persuaded to enroll in the local Barnes Theater Company as his acting abilities continued to develop, simply because it was an opportunity to get to know other people his age in the area. ('I really wasn't part of the acting fraternity at my school,' he said.) Prior to enrolling in the local theater troupe, he had sought his father's advice, looking for direction as to where he should go and what he should try to accomplish given the fact that his remaining days at Harrodian were numbered and his modeling career was at its end. 'I started doing plays when I was about fifteen or sixteen. I only did it because my dad saw a bunch of pretty girls in a restaurant and he asked them where they came from and they said drama group. He said, "Son, that is where you need to go,"' Robert revealed.

Robert took his father's advice, and has admitted that he made the move to drama in order to pursue one young woman in particular. 'I went to this drama club when I was about fifteen or sixteen specifically because a girl, who I really liked, went there and that was it. I worked backstage. I never had any intention to do it and then they did *Guys and Dolls*. I really wanted to play the Nathan Detroit part so much – just completely out of the blue. I have never sung in public or anything. I just suddenly got obsessed with it.'

But despite his efforts, Robert never did get the girl. 'She thought I was nuts when I told her after,' he said, 'so it didn't really work out. But she was the reason I actually started acting. She was the girl who I went to the drama club for.'

There would be time for girls in the future, however. Until then the local drama society offered him a chance to express himself like never before, something it appeared he truly craved, but had never been capable of in front of a photographer's camera. The acting society in Barnes was founded by actress Jean Boht, most famous for the role of Nellie Boswell in Carla Lane's comedy *Bread*, as a means of bringing together the local boys and girls in order to get them working on dramatic projects. 'When I formed the group for teenagers, we called it the Barnes Theater Group,' Boht said. And at the time Robert certainly stood out from the crowd. 'He was gorgeous, he had long curly hair. [He was] very pretty.'

Robert began to handle small tasks behind the scenes, work that would help him better understand the nature of theater production. But soon enough, Pattinson would be on stage reveling in the spotlight. 'They used to do two shows a year, and they are all great,' he said. 'So many people from there had become actors. Rusty and Ann, who are the directors, were actors themselves and were very talented. They were a very good group, and for some reason, when I finished the back-stage thing, I just decided that I should try to act.'

Robert auditioned for *Guys and Dolls*, earning a small part as a Cuban dancer. Soon, the directors cast Robert in his first leading role in Thornton Wilder's classic *Our Town*, although he admits that a series of departures thrust him into the demanding part before he was fully prepared for such a challenge. 'A bunch of people left, I was the only one still there and got the position by mistake,' he said. 'I was the only one tall enough to play the lead.'

During his time at the theater group, Robert would also meet his good friend Tom Sturridge, who was just five months older than Pattinson, and the son of Charles Sturridge, a director well known for his work on *Brideshead Revisited*, *Shackleton*, and numerous other films and TV adaptations. Since their time together in Barnes, Robert and Tom have repeatedly found themselves entrenched in a friendly rivalry, often auditioning for the same parts – from Robert's first film *Vanity Fair* to his breakout performance as Edward Cullen in the *Twilight* series. 'We go up against each other every single time,' said Robert, 'even though we look completely different.'

After Robert performed in *Our Town*, he would win the role of the diabolical Alec d'Urberville, the man responsible for the downfall of the title character in *Tess of the d'Urbervilles*. The performance would change his life and luck, leading him beyond the sleepy confines of Barnes. The play was an adaptation of Thomas Hardy's famous and penultimate novel of the same name which was first published in 1891. Most recently, the book was adapted by the BBC for their highly acclaimed 2008 series featuring Gemma Arterton, who played agent Strawberry Fields in the James Bond film *Quantum of Solace*. But in Barnes, Robert Pattinson's dramatic representation was lauded by one member of the audience who helped introduce him to the late international casting agent Mary Selway. Selway, who passed away in 2004, had a storied three-decade career casting roles for many of cinema's most renowned directors, including Steven Spielberg, Roman Polanski, Clint Eastwood, Sydney Pollack, Robert Altman and Ridley Scott. After spending time in the role of Malcolm, Prince of Scotland, in a production of Shakespeare's *Macbeth* at the Old Sorting Office Arts Center in Barnes, Robert, with Selway's assistance, would soon receive a number of professional offers.

'I can honestly say I know it would have changed his life,' Jean Boht said of Robert's time at the Barnes Theater Group. 'We had the best he could have ever hoped to be introduced to. Cooks Gordon was the National Theater production manager with Laurence Olivier. And [Gordon] was our production manager.' Even when he became part of the Barnes Theater Company, Robert was less than specific about his future desires, but the little club with the iconic green doors offered Robert a chance to accelerate his talent and obtain a first-rate agent.

Robert Pattinson was on his way, and to this day, he speculates that his father had 'some sort of weird foresight' regarding his son's career path, owing to the fact that the two of them argued for a long time over whether he should join the company. His father Richard 'nagged me about attending. At one point he said he would pay me, which is pretty strange – I don't know what his intentions were, but I went.' Robert has stated the he 'owes everything to that little club', repeating that his short time on the community stage brought him to the attention of a wider network and helped catapult him to greater fortune. Robert has also said that during those formative years, he hoped for a long, steady, successful progression in his acting career rather than disorientating overnight success. 'I remember when I was younger I used to write in my diary: I want my luck to be spread. Never give me anything too lucky all at once. I'll take a little luck now and then, but spread it for seventy years,' said Robert of a time when he was looking towards the future. 'Now that all of this [success related to *Twilight*] is happening, I'm sure the rest of my life will be ruined.'

3
Just Like Jack

'I saw *One Flew Over the Cuckoo's Nest*, and I dressed like Jack Nicholson's character.
I wanted to play that character at all times in my life.'
– Robert Pattinson

Sometimes a good film can enable a young actor to learn more about themselves than they ever expected. For Robert Pattinson, that movie was the Oscar-winning classic, *One Flew Over the Cuckoo's Nest*. This renowned adaptation of Ken Kesey's novel starred actor Jack Nicholson as Randle Patrick McMurphy, a mental patient who rebels against the despotic rules of his nurse and asylum. Nicholson had previously been nominated for the Best Actor Oscar in 1973 for *The Last Detail* and again in 1974 for *Chinatown*, but came up short on both occasions. Nicholson's performance in this 1975 drama finally earned the actor his first golden statue and is considered by some to be one of the greatest and most iconic performances in the history of modern cinema.

'I saw *One Flew Over the Cuckoo's Nest*, and I dressed like Jack Nicholson's character,' said Robert. 'I wanted to play that character at all times in my life. It didn't have anything to do with films. I just felt very uncomfortable being myself when I was younger. I just picked up different mannerisms from different movies and never really put two and two together that it was actually acting. Then I started watching a lot of Godard films. I liked the freedom in the things you could do with acting.'

Citing Nicholson as 'the reason I wanted to be an actor', Robert commented that the blithe attitude of Nicholson's character towards the world assisted him in overcoming obstacles while on stage or in front of the camera. 'I used to be so timid,' he said, 'and that was one of those films that [helped me break out] by pretending to be Randle.' Soon enough Robert had watched every one of Nicholson's films. Renowned for his brilliant portrayals of neurotic characters, Nicholson's selection of dark-edged roles would later inspire Robert to pursue indie scripts that offered him the chance to portray similarly tormented characters – Toby Jugg in *The Haunted Airman* amongst them.

'I think he is literally the only actor who I can guarantee if I see a Jack

Nicholson movie which I haven't seen, even though I've seen them all now, but it's like the same Jack Nicholson on a DVD box or whatever. It's like a seal of approval. So, you know that there's something going to be worth watching about the movie. Every single thing he's done, it's bizarre.'

But if Robert ever wanted to expand his career as his hero Nicholson had done in the past few decades, he would need contacts in the television and movie industries to help steer him beyond the confines of Barnes' close-knit acting community. Fresh from his attention-grabbing performances in *Tess of the d'Urbervilles* and *Our Town*, Robert was now ready to tackle new challenges and new roles. With Mary Selway in his corner, the young Londoner didn't have to wait long for the offers to start coming in.

Robert earned his first screen role in *Vanity Fair*, a 2004 drama starring Gabriel Byrne and the well-established, reputable Reese Witherspoon (an actress he will later be reunited with in a highly anticipated adaptation of the historical novel *Water for Elephants*). Humbled by the opportunity, Robert later recognized how dramatically his career had accelerated from a small theater in Barnes to working with an award-winning actress. (Witherspoon collected the Best Actress statuette at the 2006 Oscars for her performance as June Carter in the Johnny Cash biopic *Walk the Line*.) 'My first job I was playing Reese Witherspoon's son, and I hadn't done any acting in school,' said Robert. 'I wasn't in a drama school or anything. I'd done one amateur play, and you end up doing a film with Reese Witherspoon.'

Adapted from the famous 1848 novel by English author William Makepeace Thackeray, *Vanity Fair* explores the torrid and complex rise and fall of cynical social climber Becky Sharp (Witherspoon), from her impoverished childhood to a precarious position on the edge of the 19th-century British aristocracy. While there have been numerous television and film adaptations of the novel over the years, this version was perhaps most controversial for deviating from Thackeray's original plot, with an ending that strikes a more modest note than the one found in the novel. Directed by Mira Nair, the costume drama featured Robert Pattinson as Rawdy Crawley, the neglected son of Becky Sharp. Despite his very admirable performance, the scenes featuring Pattinson would later be edited and removed from the film's theatrical release.

Vanity Fair itself received mixed reviews, with Stephen Hunter of the *Washington Post* praising it as a 'fine movie version of the 1848 book, in all its glory and scope and wit'. Meanwhile, *Entertainment Weekly* scored the film a B-, complaining that the script 'borders on perky – a duller, safer tonal choice for the story of a conniving go-getter whose fall is as precipitous as her rise'.

Lawrence Toppman of the *Charlotte Observer* wrote, 'The cast is uniformly good, even when dealing with sudden mood changes forced by the screenwriters' need to move forward.' Of course, no one who reviewed the theatrical release had the opportunity to evaluate the performance of Robert Pattinson, as his scenes were left on the cutting-room floor. Shortly after the movie's final edit had been completed, the cast assembled for a special screening. Robert and his Barnes friend Tom Sturridge, who portrayed a young Georgy Osborne in the film, were excited to see the final product, as well as their names in the credits of a major motion picture.

'[Tom Sturridge] and I… we had scenes right next to each other and it was both our first job,' Robert said. 'We went to the screening, and we thought the whole thing was such a joke anyway, because we had no idea what we were doing. We were like, "acting" or whatever – we had no idea – and we watched [Sturridge's] scene and were like, "Yeah, that's pretty good, that's alright."'

But Pattinson was soon disappointed when he realized that his scenes had been left out of the final version. 'I'm sitting there going, "Ummm… really?" No one had told me that I had been cut out.' (It is worth noting that given Pattinson's recent prominence, newer versions of the DVD have included his 'extra scenes' in response to the rising interest in every facet of Robert's career.) The exclusion of his scenes naturally left Pattinson questioning his acting talent. At the time he may have thought that his performance was not quite up to task, especially alongside such esteemed talent. However, looking back, it has become increasingly apparent that producers were motivated by something other than doubt regarding Pattinson's performance. While the experience may have left Robert questioning his thespian skills, the reality was that the film featured a very mature-looking, seventeen-year-old Pattinson playing the son of an actress who, at various moments in the film, appeared nearly as young as he was. In real life Reese Witherspoon is only ten years older than Robert Pattinson, but she was playing his mother. As Robert himself said, 'She was twenty-seven at the time, and it was ridiculous!'

Despite not being initially credited in *Vanity Fair*, Robert still earned his first acting paycheck for his time and performance. But worth more than the wage was the fact that Robert had firmly padded his résumé with a remarkable accomplishment, sharing camera time with such an esteemed cast on his first job, while at the same time receiving praise from the *Vanity Fair* company. Witherspoon herself especially remembered Pattinson for his boyish good looks. Asked four years later what she could recall about working with the now famous Pattinson, she said, 'I remember he was *verrrrry* handsome! I was like, "I have a really handsome son!" I had to sob and cry all over him, but he was great.'

Robert relished the experience of being on set and realized that a career as a professional actor was well within his reach. As he later said, 'You have a trailer and stuff. It was the most ridiculous thing. And I was thinking, "I should be an actor. I'm doing a movie with Reese Witherspoon. How is this happening?" It's the one job where you can do whatever you want and people have got to accept it. If you were going to an office, got upset and said, "I need to go punch out some windows because I have to do this database," you'd get fired! But you get a lot of slack as an actor. You can just go nuts all the time.'

But, in truth, his career was ready to 'go nuts' all by itself. Only a few months after he completed filming *Vanity Fair*, Robert scored his first prominent role in a movie produced for German television. He had been cast for the difficult-to-pronounce role of Giselher in *Ring of the Nibelungs*. Again he was performing alongside a cast of prolific actors, including Julian Sands (with whom Robert would later reunite in *The Haunted Airman*), Max von Sydow (renowned for his performance in 1973's *The Exorcist*, one of Robert's favorite films), and Alicia Witt (whose work has spanned from *The Sopranos* to *Friday Night Lights*). 'I went to do my first big movie when I was seventeen,' said Robert of the film. 'I was in South Africa for three and a half months, and I was by myself.'

Ring of the Nibelungs is a story about a mighty blacksmith named Siegfried (portrayed by German actor Benno Fürmann), who slays a dragon and earns the heart of the warrior queen Brunnhild (played by Kristanna Loken, better known in the US as Arnold Schwarzenegger's nemesis in the *Terminator 3: Rise of the Machines*). As a reward for killing the dragon, Siegfried receives a massive treasure that turns out to possess a curse and threatens his future with Brunnhild. As Giselher, Robert Pattinson played the young brother of King Gunther and Princess Kriemhild. Giselher idolizes Siegfried as a demigod and stows himself away on a ship in order to follow on the blacksmith's quests.

Depending on the country of release, *Ring of the Nibelungs* developed several different titles over the years, including *Dark Kingdom: The Dragon King*, *Die Nibelungen*, *Curse of the Ring*, and *Sword of Xanten*.

Although it was originally produced for German television, the film also found a film or television outlet in Australia, the UK and the United States. Based on Germanic and Nordic myths, the story was influenced by many of the same legends that had inspired J.R.R. Tolkien to write *The Lord of the Rings* trilogy. Dubbed in German for German television, *Die Nibelungen*, as it was known, aired on 29 November 2004 and became the highest-rated miniseries on television that year. In the UK, it was titled *Sword of Xanten* and released theatrically, and shown on Channel Four approximately one year later.

While reviews of the film were favorable, there was once again no mention of the young Robert Pattinson, who played his role admirably. However, Robert's performance would ultimately cause a good deal of discussion; it would be the role of Giselher that ultimately created reservations about his casting in the *Twilight* series. Ironically, pictures of a young Robert dressed as Giselher the Viking later graced the landing pages of certain major websites upon announcement that he would play the role of Edward Cullen. These pictures naturally drew a wide amount of criticism as fans of the series failed to see in them a potentially handsome, chisel-jawed vampire who could truly sweep Bella off her feet. Rather, they saw a goofy Viking man-child wearing a wig, with a scruffy blonde beard and a face caked in make-up.

Despite his opportunity to travel abroad and his increased screen time in the series' four parts, Robert still needed to keep up with his studies. He would also find that new roles and success placed him in an awkward position regarding his academic future. Since his earliest days at Tower House Preparatory, he had shown a great level of indifference to school and homework. Now, his father Richard expressed doubts about paying the fees required for him to complete his A-levels, proposing that his son no longer needed to attend school given his career's acceleration. 'My dad said to me, "Okay you might as well leave since you're not working very hard." When I said I wanted to stay on for my A-levels, he said I'd have to pay my own fees, then he'd pay me back if I got good grades.' Having suddenly recognized the importance of his education – particularly since he was considering attending university – Robert accepted the offer and began to focus on achieving his A-level certificates.

In England, Northern Ireland, Wales and some parts of Scotland, students are expected to complete a series of exams at the end of their secondary education in order to receive their Advanced Level General Certificate of Education, universally referred to as an A-level. This qualification is a prerequisite for university-level study, similar to high-school graduation in the United States. While on set in South Africa, Robert maintained a strict school-work regimen, but missed a university interview due to filming commitments for the *Ring of the Nibelungs*. While phone calls from casting agents and time in front of the camera were occasional interruptions, Robert buckled down over the final months of school and performed exceptionally on his exams, receiving an A and two Bs. 'I don't know how that happened,' Robert said. 'I didn't even know half the syllabus. I lost faith in the exam system at that point.' Whether or not he truly lost his confidence in Britain's educational system, Robert had revealed his true intelligence after years of coyly disguising himself as an indifferent academic. He showed that he had the drive and intellect to potentially attend university had his acting career not produced such encouraging results.

He used his earnings from his two films and modeling contracts to pay for his final year at Harrodian. Still seventeen years old, Robert was at a crossroads. Given his outstanding A-level results, he began to consider the idea of following his sister Victoria's path and attending university. But at the same time, Mary Selway was busy working behind the scenes to arrange auditions for a number of potential roles. As Selway had helped Robert secure his part in *Vanity Fair*, it seems likely that she sought an even larger role for her protégé as a way to make up for his non-appearance in the film's final cut. Shortly before he took off for South Africa, Selway had found a potential breakthrough audition for him, one that could lead to a performance that would catapult him into the spotlight, capturing the attention of directors and producers worldwide. That role was Cedric Diggory, the doomed schoolboy in the fourth installment of the *Harry Potter* series, *Harry Potter and the Goblet of Fire*.

If he could secure this part, Robert Pattinson would be on his way from his A-levels to the A-list.

4

A Magical Ride

'Cedric exemplifies all that you would expect the Hogwarts
champion to be. Robert Pattinson was born to play the role; he's
quintessentially English with chiseled public schoolboy good looks.'
– Mike Newell, director of *Harry Potter and the Goblet of Fire*

Just prior to Robert's trip to South Africa to film *Ring of the Nibelungs*,
Mary Selway introduced the young Londoner to Mike Newell, the
director of *Harry Potter and the Goblet of Fire*. Although the meeting
was relatively informal, Selway was positioning Robert for a part in the
upcoming blockbuster. Shortly after production on the German television
film wrapped in South Africa, Robert was called for a second audition
with Newell and received his first big break.

At the age of eighteen, Robert Pattinson had passed his A-level exams,
shared camera time with Reese Witherspoon, and traveled to the far
reaches of Viking lore for his most recent project. But this latest role in the
fourth installment of the most acclaimed film series of the decade marked
his chance to catapult to instant heartthrob status. Robert had been cast
for the part of Cedric Diggory in the upcoming 2005 *Harry Potter* film.
Newell would later boast of Robert and the character: 'Cedric exemplifies
all that you would expect the Hogwarts champion to be. Robert Pattinson
was born to play the role; he's quintessentially English with chiseled public
schoolboy good looks.' With a budget set at £76 million, *Harry Potter and
the Goblet of Fire* would provide Robert with his first blockbuster role,
one that placed him among a massive cast of prominent actors, including
Harry Potter himself, Daniel Radcliffe.

Robert, however, may have been less than honest in his casting calls
with Selway and Newell. In order to land the plum role of Cedric, he
allegedly told producers that he was a big fan of soccer and snowboarding,
even though he preferred darts and swimming. Certainly, a few white
lies were only natural given the circumstances. What really mattered was
that he later recognized that casting agent Mary Selway, who passed away
around the same time the film began shooting, played a major role in
securing him the part. 'I just finished filming for the other role in South
Africa, Cape Town. I was there for three months in an apartment at just

seventeen. It was ridiculous, so I came back really confident. The casting agent on *Vanity Fair* was the same as the one on *Harry Potter* and I was the first person to be seen for any part on the film, which could have helped.'

Harry Potter and the Goblet of Fire is the fourth novel and film of J.K. Rowling's famous series. The story revolves around the boy-wizard Harry Potter as he battles the magical forces of evil – in the shape of Lord Voldemort – during the Triwizard Tournament. In the story, the threat of Lord Voldemort returns just as Harry and his classmates are entering their fourth year at Hogwarts. Voldemort's 'Dark Mark' hovers menacingly above the Quidditch World Cup Final, inciting chaos and fear amongst the school population. Back at Hogwarts, staff and students alike are frantically preparing for the Triwizard Tournament, an international competition for magicians over the age of seventeen from three famous schools: Hogwarts, Beauxbatons and Durmstrang. Contestants for the competition are chosen by the Goblet of Fire. To represent Hogwarts, the goblet selects Cedric Diggory, a sixth-year Hufflepuff student at the school of witchcraft and wizardry. In the book, Diggory is described as an exemplary student who always plays fair. Although pitted against each other in Quidditch and the Triwizard Tournament, Cedric and Harry form an important bond, growing ever closer. Initially rivals, they're soon fighting alongside each other against Voldemort, right up until the tragic moment when Cedric is murdered.

While Robert may have professed to know a thing or two about soccer and snowboarding, he admitted that, prior to his auditions, he wasn't particularly well-versed in Hogwarts tradition. 'I hadn't read any of [the *Harry Potter* books] either. I read the fourth one just before my audition in a day, and it changed my whole opinion about the whole series.' Cedric Diggory acts as an archetypal good guy; a well-liked student who enjoys the healthy competition of the Triwizard Tournament. But, outside the magical games, he's also Harry's romantic rival. 'It's impossible to hate Cedric,' Robert told the *Evening Standard*. 'He's competitive, but he's also a nice guy.' But, just as he would when later auditioning for the part of Edward Cullen, Robert initially became uncomfortable about fulfilling the role of the young, attractive wizard from Hogwarts. In the original book, as well as the first script Robert read, Cedric Diggory is described as 'an absurdly handsome seventeen-year-old'. Not only was Robert concerned about how he looked in comparison to the script's description, he also found that this paranoia affected his ability to remember his lines and remain in character. 'It kind of puts you off a little bit when you're trying to act, and you're trying to get good angles to look good-looking and stuff,' Robert said. 'It's really stupid; you'd think I'm really egotistical. But I think that's the most daunting part about it – it's much scarier than meeting Voldemort [Ralph Fiennes's character].'

Shortly before filming began, producers spelled out exactly the requirements of of J.K. Rowling's Cedric – extremely fit and extraordinarily handsome. Robert, of course, would need to meet these physical demands. 'I hadn't done anything for about six months before so I was a little bit unfit,' Robert said. 'I remember the costume designer saying when I was trying on swimming trunks, "Aren't you supposed to be fit? You could be playing a sissy poet or something."' Robert was soon paired with a personal trainer who pushed him very hard on a customized diet and exercise plan. 'Then I got a call the next day from the assistant director saying that they were putting me on a personal training program. I thought that would be pretty cool, because it would make me take it seriously. It was run by one of the stunt team, who are the most absurdly fit guys in the world. I can't even do ten press-ups. I did about three weeks of that, and in the end I think he got so bored of trying to force me to do it that he wrote it all down so that I could do it at home.' However, the training pushed Robert a bit too far. During his program, he injured his shoulder, quickly bringing his strict exercise schedule to a halt. Rather than recast the part, producers chose to accept Robert Pattinson in his current physical form as Cedric Diggory.

When the time came to begin shooting, Robert was naturally intimidated by the size of the massive cast. Feeling that he was in over his head, he began to question his own acting skills. 'On *Harry Potter* I was so conscious of the fact that I didn't know what I was doing,' Robert said. 'I used to sit on the side of the set throwing up.' The cast of prominent actors included Gary Oldman, Ralph Fiennes, Alan Rickman and Timothy Spall – all renowned for their own individual contributions to modern British cinema. Equally intimidating was the film's star, Daniel Radcliffe, who at the time had already reached the heights of international superstardom, even though he was three years younger than Pattinson. 'At first I felt a bit of pressure,' Robert said, 'but after a week, when all the cast were known, and they are all so nice, then the feeling was gone. When I was shooting my first scene, the maze scene, there was a crew of about 150 people, me, Dan and the producer. Later on, it became about 2,000 people involved in shooting. I'm really glad I could get started in a more relaxed environment and get used to it progressively.'

Although Robert was surrounded by an extraordinary number of award-winning actors, it was Michael Gambon and Warwick Davis who stood out as the most intriguing individuals on set. Gambon, who portrays Professor Dumbledore, is a seasoned Irish actor who has appeared in films such as *Gosford Park* and *Sleepy Hollow*. At three-feet-six-inches tall, Warwick Davis is best known for his role as Willow Ufgood in the 1988 epic adventure movie *Willow*. Having been a fan of the film while growing up, Robert naturally pursued a chance to seek an autograph from Davis. 'I had one scene sitting next to him at the dragon task,' Robert said, 'and I had no idea what to say to him at all. He was the only person I asked for an autograph the whole way through it.'

Robert admitted to feeling slightly star-struck when he first met the younger actors of the series, all of whom had appeared in the three films leading up to *Goblet of Fire*. As well as Daniel Radcliffe, Robert worked with Rupert Grint and Emma Watson, who played Ron Weasley and Hermione Granger. 'We did this rehearsal week and it was kind of weird meeting these three rather iconic kids, and just talking to them normally. I couldn't really get it out of my head, like, "You're Harry Potter," but that was strange, but not really, everyone was very friendly. It's a very relaxed set.' But early on, Robert worried about not fitting in. He spent most of his time stood on the sidelines for the first few days, claiming to be a famous twenty-four-year-old actor from South Africa, when in reality he was still just a teenager.

Although Robert didn't spend too much time conversing with two-time Academy-Award nominee Ralph Fiennes, he still experienced a rather amusing interaction with the famous English actor. Fiennes, who portrays the evil Lord Voldemort, is perhaps best known for his performances in *Quiz Show*, *The English Patient* and *In Bruges*, as well as nearly forty other films. 'I didn't really talk to Ralph Fiennes while I was doing *Harry Potter* and the only thing I did with him was when he stepped on my head,' Pattinson said. 'Then I went to this play and he was there. And this girl said, "You've worked with Ralph Fiennes haven't you, Robert?" And I was like, "Well, no…" and Ralph said, "Yes, I stepped on your head." And that was the extent of our conversation.'

But while interactions with the cast weren't always easy for the young actor, his participation in stunts and special effects would provide additional challenges he'd never experienced in his earlier productions. Although he'd worked with a small special-effects crew in *Ring of the Nibelungs*, Robert recognized that working with some 2,000 people

Previous page: *Before he was famous:*
Robert has one of his first red-carpet experiences
at the UK premiere of The Dukes of Hazzard *in*
August 2005 – Harry Potter *arrived in*
cinemas three months later.

Above left: *Come on, give us a smile!*
The blonde-locked Robert in his early days
at Tower House.

Above right: *Treading the boards with*
the Barnes Theater Group.

Above left: *Rob releases his inner reptile for another teen photo shoot.*

Above right: *Rob as Cedric Diggory in* Harry Potter, *a role director Mike Newell said the young actor was 'born to play'.*

Above: *Mystery man: With the cast of* Harry
Potter and the Goblet of Fire, *October 2005.
While filming, Rob claimed to be a famous
twenty-four-year-old actor from South Africa,
though he was just seventeen.*

Opposite: *Widely touted as 'the next Jude Law',
Robert smolders at the London premiere of* Harry
Potter and the Goblet of Fire, *2005.*

Above left: *Arachnophobes need not apply: Robert plays tormented RAF pilot Toby Jugg in 2006 chiller* The Haunted Airman.

Above right: *Just strumming along: gifted guitarist Rob still laughs about his role as a struggling musician named Art in the indie film* How to Be *(2008).*

Opposite: *Different strokes . . . Robert spurned traditional heartthrob roles in favor of the chance to portray painter Salvador Dali in* Little Ashes *(2008).*

Overleaf: *Waking up to success? A stubbly-faced Robert shows off an early version of his trademark windswept locks at the New York premiere of* Harry Potter, *November 2005.*

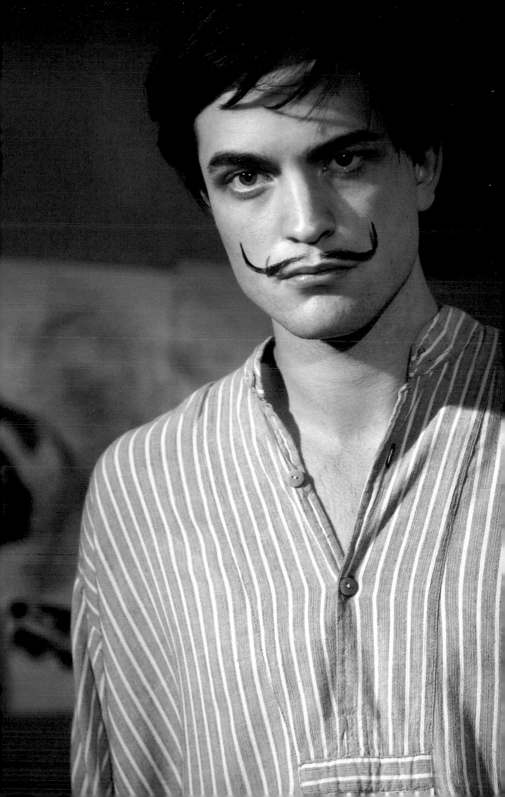

on the *Goblet of Fire* set would prove to be a very different experience. Perhaps the most memorable scene for Robert was the 'maze' scene during the Triwizard Tournament's third task. Robert described the experience as 'enforced method acting', meaning there was no need to fake any excitement and tension during filming. 'We were really hyped up,' he said. 'You are on 100 percent adrenaline and you're starting this in the first week and you have just met all the other actors the week before and now you have to go crazy with them. That was pretty intense, but I think it was really the most fun, because it was really physical work.' The physical side of *Harry Potter* posed a unique challenge that would push Robert to his limits. In one scene of the movie, Cedric Diggory competes in an underwater task – calling for Robert to undertake a crash course in scuba diving during his first week on set. 'I had never done scuba diving before,' he said. 'I was in a tiny little tub that was a practice tank. I didn't see the big tank until they first started shooting in it. It was about a hundred times the size of the practice tank and it was so much deeper, so that was sort of scary when I first got there, because you have to get used to all the pressure and things like that. It is completely blue in there and there are divers with breathing equipment that are completely blue as well. You can't really see anything. You just get this breather put into your mouth after the take has been done. I got used to it quickly though.

'It's a very physical part; the stuff in the maze which was done in the beginning was all on huge action sets. The hedges were huge and hydraulically operated. I got hit by stuff, getting pulled around by ropes, and Dan and I were running around punching each other so it was kind of vicious! There was a lot of underwater stuff which I quite liked; it got therapeutic after a while.'

Cedric Diggory's untimely demise occurred towards the end of the movie, bringing Robert's brief *Harry Potter* career to a fittingly dramatic conclusion. Due to it featuring the death of such an admirable character, the film is viewed by fans and critics alike as much darker than its three predecessors. Robert himself conceded that it may be a bit too dark for young children given that the script followed the book so closely. However, he pointed out that, 'Your imagination is more terrifying than a film could ever be, and I think they're ready to see this side of the franchise.' Reflecting on Diggory's death scene, in which the champion is killed by Peter Pettigrew (Timothy Spall) and Lord Voldemort, Pattinson said, 'We redid it three times I think, because Ralph Fiennes could only shoot on certain days. So me and Dan tried to get bits of it done without him, and when he came – because of the way the last bits were shot with Voldemort – a lot of it had to be rearranged, and so it was strange because the first time I shot it I had about a month off through January, and so I sort of psyched myself up to do this scene, and then when we reshot it I think we were filming the Yule Ball at the same time . . . it was exciting.'

Harry Potter and the Goblet of Fire ignited fans' passion for the franchise and Robert's performance certainly stood out. 'I read the *Variety* review and their only comment was "rangy",' he said. 'I thought it meant from the range, like a cowboy. But it just means tall and lanky.' However, at the premiere of *Harry Potter and the Goblet of Fire*, fans showed Robert that an actor can indeed become a star overnight. 'The day before [the film was released] I was just sitting in Leicester Square, happily being ignored by everyone. Then suddenly strangers are screaming your name. Amazing.'

When Robert spoke of movie premieres it was with more than a little trepidation, anticipating his future reservations about the massive hype surrounding *Twilight*. 'I've been to a couple of Warner Brothers film premieres in the last few weeks,' he said, 'and considering no one knows who I am, it's still a pretty scary event. So I don't know what it's gonna be like when you actually have to do something rather than just walk in. I still trip over my feet and stuff when I'm not supposed to be doing anything. So I'll just see how it goes. I'm looking forward to it.'

For Robert himself, *Harry Potter* marked the first 'huge step and a massive event in my life'. That the overwhelming experience of being catapulted into the limelight and onto the red carpet affected him in such a way is, perhaps, hardly surprising. In the wake of various positive reviews, the *Times* named Robert Pattinson one of their People of the Year with an accompanying headline that read 'Almost Famous'. Patricia Dobson, the compiler of *Screen International*'s list of British Stars of Tomorrow, wrote, 'This fresh-faced, photogenic nineteen-year-old so oozed charm and likability that casting directors are predicting a big future.' Robert's breakthrough role had launched him into the world of gossip magazines and fan idolization, riding the tails of one of the largest franchises in cinema history. But for all of the fame, the fortune and the opportunity that lay before him, he would soon make a series of unusual career decisions that suggested he wasn't yet ready for the spotlight, or maybe even that he wanted nothing to do with it.

5

Summertime in London

'I didn't do anything for a year. I just sat on a roof and played music . . .
it was like the best time I had ever had.'
– Robert Pattinson

Shortly after his blockbuster debut in *Harry Potter and the Goblet of Fire*, Flora Stubbs of the *London Evening Standard* predicted a rapid ascendancy for Robert Pattinson not seen since another young Londoner – and winner of the 'Most Promising Newcomer' award – caused a similar sensation in the 1997 biopic *Wilde*. 'Robert Pattinson, nineteen, is being dubbed "the next Jude Law" for a screen-stealing performance as the dashing head boy in *Harry Potter and the Goblet of Fire*,' wrote Stubbs. 'The London-born teenager, who plays Potter's love rival, will set hearts racing among female cinema goers when the film is released this month.' It was quite a comparison, especially given that Robert was only appearing in his first major-budget production and playing a relatively minor role in the massively successful *Harry Potter* franchise. (Additionally, at the time the comparison was made, Jude Law had a receding hairline and relationship scandals to address, while Robert Pattinson was an eligible young bachelor whose windswept brown locks were fast becoming a trademark look. This might have prompted Judith Finnigan of UK talk show *Richard and Judy* to compare him to a younger Orlando Bloom, while in the same breath gushing that Rob was 'one of the most gorgeous young men I have ever seen'.)

Although Pattinson's character perishes in the film, he had certainly garnered a great deal more attention than first anticipated, and was set to make a return in a dreamlike sequence in *Harry Potter and the Order of the Phoenix*, the next installment of the series. This brief reappearance of his character would only remind fans of his boyish good looks and lead to further praise. Given the hype, his agent Stephanie Ritz at Endeavor Talent Agency was eager to find Pattinson a high-profile role in another big-budget film, one that would propel him into the same class as Jude Law or Daniel Radcliffe.

But Pattinson had become increasingly cautious about his long-term aspirations. Prior to filming *Harry Potter*, he had seriously considered going back to full-time education to pursue a trade, possibly reigniting his passion for political communications. 'I was always intending to go to university,' said Robert. 'But *Harry Potter* went to overtime, so I didn't have to think about going to university. I just fell into acting and then after I'd finished that movie, I was like, "Oh well, I guess I'm an actor now."'

Robert bounced around Los Angeles for a short period following the film, praising the laidback, somewhat impersonal feel of Hollywood. 'I like meetings there [in LA],' he said of his early experiences in Tinseltown. 'You go in, no one cares if you're a nice person or not. You just do it, and if you can do it, you do it, and if you can't, you can't.' It was a very fair summary of life in Hollywood, a town where good looks and a handshake might get you far, but connections, perfect auditions and the gut feelings of casting directors had become more important. Robert was finding that he wasn't really acquiring the roles and opportunities that would test him as an actor, instead being offered parts that were reserved for teen heartthrobs. He soon moved back to London and into a small flat in the trendy area of Soho. He rented the apartment, which he described as a 'cool little ex-crack den', with Barnes friend Tom Sturridge. It was, perhaps, a radical departure from his high-profile performance in *The Goblet of Fire*. But for an actor trying to better understand his craft, and for a young man with a passion for music, Soho was a perfect landing zone after the hectic pace of the past few months. 'It was so cool,' Robert said of his London apartment. 'You had to walk through a restaurant kitchen to get up to the roofs . . . I didn't do anything for a year. I just sat on a roof and played music . . . it was like the best time I had ever had.'

Having played the guitar and piano from an early age, Robert still harbored a restless desire to jump back into music, and soon found himself playing at London's Up All Night Music, a popular open-microphone night that producer Phil Taylor had built from the ground up. During this time, Robert befriended a number of local musicians, hanging out at bars until the early hours with a new group of friends that Taylor called the 'Brit Pack'. (The term is adapted from the immensely popular 'Brat Pack', a group of young American actors and actresses who frequently appeared together in teen-oriented coming-of-age films in the 1980s.)

'We spent the better part of a year just getting drunk every night,' Robert said. The group of friends, with whom Robert would later collaborate on a number of tracks for the *Twilight* soundtrack, included musicians Bobby Long, Marcus Foster, and Sam Bradley, as well as his actor roommate Tom Sturridge. (Just a few years later, for *Twilight*, Bradley co-wrote the song 'Never Think' with Pattinson, while Long and Foster wrote the film's bonus track 'Let Me Sign').

It was clear that Robert was enjoying the late-night sessions, while his interest in big-budget films had cooled significantly. Several miles from Robert's hometown of Barnes rests Soho, a lively entertainment district with a popular music scene that can be traced back to 1948. The area is a heaving maze of unique venues and quaint, popular bars in which Robert could forget about his public image and indulge in a little late-night revelry. He also relished the difference in tempo between Los Angeles, a city dominated by the machinations of the movie industry, and the arguably more cosmopolitan London, where locals adopted a laidback attitude towards actors and musicians who stayed up late, drinking pints and writing songs. 'In England, if you want to look rough you go out and get really drunk and come in looking really hungover,' he said, 'but if you do that in America it's like, "Have you got a drinking problem?"'

At the time that he and his friends were writing music, Robert showed an unbridled commitment to the guitar and piano, consistently arriving at the open-mic nights in order to play with his band Bad Girls. In fact, Pattinson wasn't exactly candid with the Brit Pack about his acting career. 'I had no idea that Robert was an actor,' said Phil Taylor. 'I just knew that he is a great musician and a very good singer-songwriter. I had probably known Marcus and Rob for about a year or so when I introduced them to Bobby [Long].'

Robert was beginning to question his ability to continue down the acting path and might well have been considering a full-time transition into music. However, he soon recognized that technology was having an adverse effect on anyone trying to make a living as a musician, and his concerns about the music industry's seeming decline affected his ability to fully commit to songwriting. His sister Lizzy, for example, had gone from atop the international charts to selling music off of her MySpace page in just a few years. Given the rise of file-sharing websites that allowed people to download music illegally, Robert didn't see being a musician as an economically viable career.

'I used to want to be a musician before I kind of fell into acting,' he said. 'I wanted to be a pianist – doing the kind of Tom Waits thing was my ideal. But I guess since the advent of Kazaa and all these download things, it's impossible to make any money out of music whatsoever. So I've never really pursued it as a career.'

Living in Soho, Robert could set his own pace. But, much like any other trade, his acting required some level of education and training, which Robert felt he had never formally received up to this point. Although he had taken classes in speech at Tower House, worked his way from stagehand to leading man at the Barnes Theater Group, and portrayed a character central to the storyline of one of the largest film franchises in cinema history, Robert felt he'd never truly learned how to be a professional actor. If he meant to pursue a career in this field, he would have to instruct himself, adopting the same entrepreneurial spirit upon which the Pattinson household was founded.

'After *Harry Potter*, I sort of tried to teach myself to act because I didn't learn in school or anything.' He began by turning down the easy roles being pitched to him by Stephanie Ritz, parts that could have provided an easy paycheck and landed him on the cover of every gushing Hollywood magazine. Pattinson was choosing the hard road to success, and it seemed that the more obscure the script, the greater the draw for the young actor. While Robert may have been uncertain about his direction, this kind of experimentation was a luxury he could afford for an extended period of time. With a steady flow of income from royalties and other payments for his *Harry Potter* role, he could enjoy the downtime, seeking out projects that he found edgy and personally fulfilling.

He made up his mind to return to the stage, a familiar place for the young man who started out treading the boards of Barnes Theater. In May 2005, Robert was slated to appear in the UK premiere of a German play entitled *The Woman Before* at the Royal Court Theater. The Royal Court is based in London's West End – considered the equivalent of Broadway in New York – and, according to press releases, it is 'Britain's leading national company dedicated to new work by innovative writers from the UK and around the world'. The theater also claims to be the producer of 'more new plays than any other theater in Britain'. Robert was naturally proud to have been cast by such a prestigious company. 'At the time I really thought, "Wow, I must be great, I'm like fucking Brando!"' Pattinson joked of his move to theater after such a high-profile film. 'I had this specific idea where, "I'm going to be a weirdo, this is how I'm going to promote myself." And then of course I ended up getting fired.'

Over the years, tabloids and fans alike have speculated on what went on behind the scenes, hinting at a number of reasons for Pattinson's sacking from the production, but Robert's own words seem to indicate a falling out between himself and members of the production team over his interpretation of the character. Considering Robert's vision of Edward Cullen would be the source of similar disagreements with writers and members of the *Twilight* team years later, his version of events comes as no surprise. 'I did a play which I got fired from in the West End, and I realized I needed to learn some of the fundamentals – like how to act,' Robert shrugged, determined to learn from the incident.

In a later interview with Ruben Nepales for *You* magazine, Rob suggested that he had been 'fired from that play' because of his maverick approach. 'I liked the freedom in the things you could do with acting,' he explained. 'Like if you want to look sad, you don't have to have a sad face, which is still how I try on a lot of different things. For that same reason – trying to take risks – I got fired from that play. I haven't really changed since I got fired.'

Still, Robert never looked back upon the sacking as a black mark on his professional development. 'It's probably one of the best things that ever happened to me. I got some jobs afterward, by saying I got fired and for standing up for what I believe in,' Robert said with a laugh. In other accounts of the run-up to the play's opening, it was claimed that he pulled out shortly before the first performance because of illness or exhaustion following the *Harry Potter* film. Whatever the case, Robert's stint on stage was not to be. Replaced by actor Tom Riley, Robert soon turned his attention back to film and television. Whether he was sacked or voluntarily pulled out of the production, the question now was: would it harm his chances of becoming a future star?

Initially it seemed that this might be the case, as his next few appearances were in obscure productions that failed to appeal to wide audiences. Robert would only star in one production in 2006. For his first role away from *Harry Potter*, he chose a character so radically different from Cedric Diggory that it seemed like a deliberate attempt to avoid being typecast as a teen heartthrob. Could Robert have made it his goal to perform roles that were far outside the mainstream, just like his idol Jack Nicholson? The 2006 role in question was Toby Jugg in *The Haunted Airman*, a film written and directed by Chris Durlacher and based on Dennis Wheatley's chilling novel, *The Haunting of Toby Jugg*. In the lead role of Jugg, Robert played a Royal Air Force pilot who is wounded while participating in the bombing of Dresden, Germany, towards the end of World War Two, and subsequently experiences horrific post-traumatic stress. Confined to a wheelchair for the story's duration, the character is sent to a remote hospital in Wales to recover under the watch of his aunt and a psychiatrist.

There, he begins suffering from horrific dreams and hallucinations that lead him to question his sanity.

'I play a World War Two pilot who gets shot and paralyzed,' Pattinson said. 'He gets terrible shellshock and basically goes insane. It's a great part. I was in a wheelchair all the time, which is always good, just chain-smoking throughout the entire film.' In the film, Pattinson co-starred alongside Julian Sands, a fellow cast member from his second film *Ring of the Nibelungs*, and Rachael Stirling, an experienced television actress. But the cast, like the budget, was small; the part distinctly somber; and although the film was a low-key project for a young man on hiatus from Hollywood, it garnered a relatively tiny audience on BBC Four, which, at the time of its airing in 2006, was a digital channel without a significant audience reach.

Still, Pattinson's harrowing performance impressed critics. Sarah Hughes of the *Observer* wrote, 'Robert Pattinson gives an astonishingly good performance as the eponymous Toby, a crippled airman tormented by both war flashbacks and remorse. His sinister doctor Hal (a suitably menacing Julian Sands) attempts to get to the bottom of Jugg's guilt and to his relationship with his aunt Julia (Rachael Stirling). This is a somber, chilly and utterly absorbing adaptation, but two words of warning: fans of the novel should note there are differences in the plot, and arachnophobes should probably steer clear altogether.'

The *Stage* lauded Pattinson for both his portrayal and, predictably, his ravishing good looks. They wrote, 'All of the BBC's blue filters must have been requisitioned for *The Haunted Airman*, a very disturbing, beautifully made and satisfyingly chilling ghost story. Pattinson – an actor whose jaw line is so finely chiseled it could split granite – played the airman of the title with a perfect combination of youthful terror and world weary cynicism.'

Additional reviews raved as much about his looks as his outstanding performance. While the *Independent on Sunday* panned the film for its editing and terrifying visions of spiders, the review said the film was 'saved from inadequacy by the bone structure of the airman (Robert Pattinson). He was playing a character called Toby Jugg, but he sure didn't look like one . . . he was so beautiful that you kept watching.'

Robert's performance had added an impressive notch to his résumé and offered the dark, indie feel of which he was becoming fond. Still, he needed to attract larger audiences if he wanted to return to Hollywood on his own terms.

While *The Haunted Airman* might have looked like the perfect transitional role for Pattinson at the time, his next film signaled a dreadful decision on his part. Robert turned further away from Hollywood when he accepted a bizarre role in *The Bad Mother's Handbook*, a British film made for ITV that possibly generated even more poor reviews than it did viewers. A garbled, socially confused mishmash about teenage pregnancy, Alzheimer's patients and identity crises, *The Bad Mother's Handbook* could potentially have sunk Pattinson's career had *Harry Potter and the Order of the Phoenix* not flashed back to his role as Cedric Diggory at around the same time. Adapted from Kate Long's novel and released in 2007, *The Bad Mother's Handbook* was originally planned as a showcase for actress Catherine Tate. But aside from Tate, there were no other big-name actors, and the production went largely unnoticed.

The Bad Mother's Handbook is a slapstick comedy centering on the life of Charlotte Cooper, played by Holly Grainger. In the story, Charlotte is dumped by her boyfriend only to find out she is pregnant. She soon develops family problems with her mother and grandmother, but is blessed with the friendship of Daniel Gale, played by Robert. Gale is a clumsy, mumbling geek who hides behind black-framed glasses and unkempt hair (which hung over Robert's face for most of the film). He eventually develops feelings for Charlotte and becomes an emotional lifeline for her as she deals with the pregnancy and her emerging family problems.

In the film, Robert's character wears a shaggy bowl haircut and glasses that make him look like a grungy hopeful who'd auditioned for the part of Harry Potter in the wizard's college years . . . and failed. It was clearly an effort on Robert's part to downplay his good looks, widen his range, and be taken seriously in the role he was portraying. Unfortunately the film's critics were not buying this approach.

'The slapstick comedy is not working. It is clearly obvious that this is not a nerdy man,' said critic Mark Eccleston. 'It's a beautiful man with some tank tops on and funny hair and bottle glasses. And you just don't know where it's going to go. And even in the end of the film, they don't even afford him a crystal-esque, beautiful butterfly moment. He's just still odd. What they were thinking about casting him, I do not know.'

Scathing reviews swarmed newspapers and websites. Kevin Maher of the *Times* wrote that *The Bad Mother's Handbook* was 'heavily packed, if not burdened with excess dramatic incident . . . the story itself seemed practically allergic to narrative downtime – in ninety minutes there was unwanted pregnancy, adoption, manslaughter, near death, birth, romance, fights and a slightly cloying resolution.' John Preston of the *Sunday Telegraph* called it a 'mess of a drama', while Ally Ross of the *Sun* saved quite a bit of ink by narrowing the review down to one word: 'Rubbish'.

Reviews of Pattinson's performance were no more complimentary. Katie Toms of the *Observer* said: 'Floppy-haired Daniel [was] played with a little too much bumbling gusto by Robert Pattinson.' While Brian Viner at the *Independent* labeled Robert's character a 'hunchback, without the hunch'. There is little doubt that *The Bad Mother's Handbook* received the type of reviews that could have splintered Robert's career and sent him into an abyss from which he would never return. But Robert remained modest, looking back on his time after *Harry Potter* and realizing indie films were more about work and development than garnering standout reviews. 'I kind of blew it after the *Potter* films,' he said. 'There was a chance for me to really kick on and use the exposure, but I didn't really want to do anything. Looking back, it was a good thing. I was able to teach myself how to act for a start. I could have done some more teen movies, but I thought what is the point? I'm not all that fussed by making loads of money.'

Far better for his career was the brief flashback resurrection of Cedric Diggory in 2007's *Harry Potter and the Order of the Phoenix*. While there was no additional filming for Robert to undertake, given his character's murder, the role kept Pattinson's name in the spotlight. It was a fitting character to parallel Robert Pattinson's career at this time. In a eulogy of Cedric Diggory delivered in *Harry Potter and the Goblet of Fire*, Albus Dumbledore tells the students of Hogwarts to cherish the memory of the brave and big-hearted Cedric.

Robert Pattinson himself had chosen not to take the easy path to worldwide fame, shunning the typecast roles traditionally reserved for young heartthrobs. Because of his decisions to make low-budget films against the recommendations of his agents, he was finding his performances criticized in major newspapers and largely unnoticed by the general public.

If ever Robert Pattinson experienced a low point during his remarkably successful career thus far, he reached it shortly after the universal panning of *The Bad Mother's Handbook*. But Robert's response was to continue his personal odyssey into the world of indie films, where – mentally, at least – he couldn't be much further away from the lights and glamour of Hollywood and its blockbusters. If he maintained this direction, the question was: although fans would remember Cedric Diggory, would anyone remember Robert Pattinson?

6

Indie Peaks and Valleys

'I didn't want to get stuck in pretty, public-school roles,
or I knew I'd end up as some sort of caricature.'
– Robert Pattinson

After the panning of *The Bad Mother's Handbook*, it would not have been surprising if Robert had returned to Hollywood in order to pursue the heartthrob roles that casting directors and his agent wished he'd accepted following the *Harry Potter* film. However, being stubborn and committed to learning his craft, Robert continued to chase low-budget films that offered the opportunity to research and develop complex characters. Looking back, his next two roles after the critical misstep that *The Bad Mother's Handbook* represented were relatively unremarkable, yet both exhibited Robert's desire to continue on the path towards indie success. The first was the part of Richard in *The Summer House*, an independent British film written by Ian Beck (best known for writing *The Secret History of Tom Trueheart, Boy Adventurer*) and directed by Daisy Gili, a founder of the London Film Academy. 'Our script supervisor recommended Robert Pattinson to work with us mainly because he thought [Robert] could take direction well,' said director Gili. 'He wasn't too big for his own boots even though he was twenty and had a relative amount of success. And obviously he had cheekbones that you could cut steak on.'

Within the film's incredibly simple plot, Robert would only appear twice. Richard, a groveling, egotistical boyfriend (played by Pattinson), follows his girlfriend Jane (Talulah Riley) to France to try to win back her heart after a bout of infidelity. 'Robert's role in *The Summer House* film is to play this character, who isn't a particularly nice character,' said Gili. 'Actually, he's not really that interested in love. He's probably more interested in the fact that she's walked away from him.'

According to the film's official notes, the character of Richard is 'a good-looking boy, with an ambivalent feminine side, skinny and androgynous in the fashion of that time'. Writer Beck describes him as 'narcissistic' and 'the kind of boy who will hang around looking pitiful and hoping his moodiness will attract girls, which it does'. It was certainly a fitting match from a casting perspective, one that, despite the size of the role, was suggestive of future success for Robert given his ability to stand out among the unknown cast. 'I think he had a real hunger to get the acting right. He really, really worked hard at it,' commented Gili. 'We caught him at the right time, but I'm not surprised in the slightest that Catherine Hardwicke [director of *Twilight*] saw him and thought, "Wow."'

Though it was an incredibly minor role for an actor still tied to the immensely popular *Harry Potter* franchise, Robert showed tremendous poise and humility on the set, making no demands from the low-budget production and aiming only to portray his character admirably. 'Robert came out to France with us for the entire week of the shoot, even though he was only in two scenes,' said Gili. 'He did us the good service of sharing a room with the camera operator. He wasn't paid very much, if anything at all. He was an absolute treat to have on set.' At the time of writing, *The Summer House* is yet to be released, although trailers can be found on a number of online video sites. The film is expected to enter a small festival circuit and will be released via iTunes and DVD in October 2010.

Robert's next project was a similar style of film; but at least this time he would be placed in a lead role with more than just two scenes. *How to Be* is a story about a failing musician named Art (Pattinson), who, after a number of personal setbacks and recent heartbreak, moves back home with his neglectful parents (played by Rebecca Pidgeon and Michael Irving). Art soon decides to use inheritance money to pay for Canadian self-help guru, Doctor Levi Ellington (Powell Jones), to come to his home in England and help Art navigate his quarter-life crisis. 'He's kind of, I guess you'd call him a mediocrity,' Robert said of his character. 'He doesn't really fit into any kind of people grouping. He's not particularly depressed, but he thinks he is. He doesn't have any kind of consistency in his emotions, which is how I think most people are.' Despite the lack of support from his parents, Art attempts – with the help of his new life coach and two slightly neurotic friends, Nikki (Mike Pearce) and Ronny (Johnny White) – to find a balance in his life and to create a lasting relationship with his parents. 'I love the script so much,' Robert said shortly after filming. '[It's] very different from everything I read. And the ending – I love it so much.'

Director Oliver Irving naturally praised Robert's knack for giving his all during a performance, stating, 'Rob definitely comes alive when the cameras roll. His performance is always heightened by pressure – in rehearsals he would often say, "Okay, it's not right now, but I know what is needed and I'll get it on the day." This took an awful lot of faith in him but he was true to his word. He responds very well to direction and was also very up for contributing.' The role was a natural fit for Pattinson, and despite his worry that he'd missed out on formal acting training, it was his ability to improvise that made him such an asset to the production. 'Robert walked into the audition and reminded me of people I know,' said Irving. 'I think he forgot his lines and just started improvising, which is exactly what I wanted – someone who could just become the character and leave behind the kind of "techniques" trained in at drama schools. I had a hunch he would work well with [the] other cast [members] and would be able to get across the kind of naivety inherent to Art's character.'

At a time when there was so much uncertainty in Rob's own life – torn between two paths, whether he'd pursue a career in acting or music was anyone's guess – he saw a number of parallels between himself and the main character. 'It's just kind of feeling you don't really know where you're going in the world. At the time I thought that – I didn't know if I wanted to be an actor, I didn't know what I was doing, I hadn't been to university. I was bumming around, not feeling particularly good at anything but at the same time desperately wanting to and thinking, "You'll never reach your own goals you set for yourself."'

Ironically, the script also called for the musically talented Robert Pattinson to portray a mediocre musician. Given that Art sings and plays the guitar inadequately, Robert admitted that faking poor musicianship was one of the most difficult challenges in fulfilling the role. 'It's funny because it's quite difficult to fake playing the guitar really badly when you know how to play it,' said Robert. 'It was one of the most difficult parts [of the role]. It was quite fun though. I liked doing the scenes where he was doing open mics. I've been to a lot of open mics in my life and just seeing how bad some of the people are, and being one of those people who makes everyone in the audience leave.'

How to Be assembled a small cast on an even smaller budget. Still, the film garnered positive reviews from the limited number of critics who were able to view it upon release. Due to Robert's fame post-*Twilight*, certain media outlets eventually picked up and broadcasted the film, including TMF, a subsidiary of MTV, and IFC. The former offered glowing praise, specifically highlighting Pattinson's performance. 'There are good things going for *How to Be*,' the TMF reviewer wrote. 'One is you get this feeling that the filmmakers and everyone involved did not do it for the money, but to give us a good story, with characters rich and funny and honest and, most of all, just like us. There are no heroes here, nor are we forced to make believe. And you'll get to see Robert Pattinson as an emerging actor with such potential – you will simply want to watch more and more of his films.'

For his efforts, Robert was awarded 'Best Actor 2008' at the Strasbourg Film Festival for *How to Be*, and was ranked Number 23 on Moviefone's 'The 25 Hottest Actors Under 25'. His performance as Art offered him legitimacy on the indie scene, expunging memories of the failure of *The Bad Mother's Handbook* once and for all. Still, after a succession of small-budget roles, Robert Pattinson was still living in London, thumbing his guitar at open-mic nights and trying to make sense of his future career. Asked why he was avoiding big-budget films, Robert explained the thinking behind his careful choice of roles. 'Mainly because when most films are being made now they're designing it to make money even before it's started shooting. Prejudging an audience is completely impossible to do. "Audiences bought this so they're going to like this." It's impossible to do. But you're going to make the same movie again and again. No one's going to break out of it. I just thought, "I don't want to be adding shit to the pile so I might as well complain about it and not be part of it."'

Certainly Robert was not hostile to the practice of acting itself. Acting is in his blood – this much has been clear since his early roles in the Barnes Theater Group. He was simply wary of the business practices employed by large Hollywood production houses that only sought blockbuster scripts, studiously avoiding the artsy films that had grown close to his heart. After *How to Be*, Robert received a great deal of praise from independent filmmakers. Recognized as a serious actor with a disarming charm and natural humility around the set, he became someone whom many directors sought for leading roles. A number of writers and directors sent Pattinson scripts in the hope of sparking the young actor's interest. Producer Carlo Dusi had met Robert during an audition a few years prior, and pursued him for an upcoming film entitled *Little Ashes*. The opportunity would prove to be the turning point that Robert had been searching for, reigniting the confidence and love for acting that had begun to fade after *Harry Potter*.

'Robert had been on my radar for some time,' said Dusi, 'as I had actually got him to read for a role in a pilot for a feature film that I made in 2006, and while he was too young for that particular role I had already been extremely impressed by his screen presence and his acting ability. When our dates for the shoot of *Little Ashes* were confirmed and we went back into the market to find our Salvador Dali in Britain, he was immediately one of our shortlist, and his reading for the role left us all in no doubt that he was the right person for the role. Of course no one could have imagined at the time how his career would have soared so soon after our shoot, but we could all tell that there was a very special quality to him, as well as huge talent and integrity as an actor.'

Based on the life of surrealist painter Salvador Dali, *Little Ashes* was a £1.4 million-budget film and Robert's chance to work with a large cast in Spain. 'When I took it, I didn't know much about Dali. It was a good script and it was shooting in various different areas of Spain, which was a bonus. I knew very little about [Dali], but I knew from seeing videos of him when he's older that he's obviously kind of an extrovert. I hadn't played that kind of a character before, so that was appealing. I researched tons and I wound up finding a lot of stuff that I liked about him just as a man, not necessarily as an artist.'

Sharing its title with one of Dali's paintings, *Little Ashes* was an intriguing production in which Robert had originally been cast as another character – the main supporting role of Lorca. 'I was attached to that for about, I guess, two years and I was initially going to play Federico Garcia Lorca [Dali's friend and lover],' said Robert. 'And somehow, I don't know what happened. They asked me to read for Dali, and that was about a year after. It took ages to get this film made. It was a really interesting script, and about a year after I was in mind for Lorca I read for Dali, and about a year after that they suddenly said, "Oh, we've got money, we're doing it in Spain, and it starts in four days!" So I came and I just thought it would be kind of fun, I mean, you know the stuff Dali makes, kind of crazy, and I thought it would be quite fun to do.'

Early on, Robert seems to have been under the impression that the Dali story was going to be a simple project, requiring no real depth or exploration. But he soon found that Dali's existence was extraordinarily complicated, and that a full study into the life of the famous and eccentric painter would be required of him. 'I [initially] wanted to have a vacation in Spain,' Robert said. 'But it became just – really, really hard. I'd never done a job that was so hard.' Having become the star of the film, Robert certainly welcomed the challenge of crafting the Dali character, despite the heavy research required. In a move that pre-empted the exhaustive preparation he would undertake for *Twilight*, Robert spent months alone in Spain working on the look and emotional depths of the character, even though he could not speak any Spanish.

'I couldn't speak to anyone the whole time,' Robert said. 'And so I just sat over this Dali stuff. I just read and read and read, and it was one of the most satisfying jobs I've ever done because it was the one time that I really had zero distractions. It really changed my whole attitude toward acting. And it was a tiny, tiny film, which I don't think anyone will ever see, probably. But it was very interesting. Especially since I don't look anything like Dali. But at the end of the job, I kind of did look like him.'

Salvador Dali, the artist and main character of the story, was born in Figueres in Catalonia, Spain, in 1904, and died, at the age of eighty-four, in his hometown in 1989. Predominantly known as a surrealist painter – a style of art which originated when he was a teenager – he also made significant international contributions to theater, fashion, photography and more. Given his talent in a multitude of creative areas, the artist was noted for once boasting, 'Every morning upon awakening, I experience a supreme pleasure: that of being Salvador Dali.' *Little Ashes* begins by examining the life of an eighteen-year-old Dali. He travels to early-1920s Madrid and moves into the Residencia de Estudiantes (Student Halls of Residence), where he meets filmmaker Luis Buñuel and poet Federico Garcia Lorca. There he experiments in new forms of art while his friendship with the prominent male poet soon turns to love. But as Lorca becomes more obsessed with him over time, Dali decides to move to Paris. Seduced by the decadence of high society, he eventually finds himself entangled in a love triangle between a married woman obsessed with his celebrity status, and his homosexual lover.

As Robert would find while researching the part, Dali was a complex man, with a tally of unusual traits to his name. According to Dali's writings, he contradicted himself on a regular basis. 'When he was younger, if you read his autobiographical stuff – he wrote three autobiographies which completely contradict each other,' said Robert. 'There are chapters called "Truth" and other ones are called "Lies" . . . it's just really funny. There was so much about him that I found fascinating. He was an incredibly complex person. I'm not saying that I am. I'm not at all.' Given that Robert did not look or act like Dali at the time he read the script, he would need to spend a great deal of time mastering the esoteric mannerisms of the famous artist. Robert began by examining Dali's writings and photographs. 'I had this whole series of photos,' he said. 'And figured out the way he would move his body. There's a picture of him pointing. I spent days trying to figure out, "How did he get his arm like that?" It was the first time that I ever really got into characterization, trying to work on movements. I was doing tons of stuff on his walk and such. It was probably unnecessary, but it was the one time I felt, like, slightly satisfied. But I wanted to bring that intensity to every job.'

Robert's immersion in the role and finely executed research truly brought the character to life. The further he delved into Dali's life, the greater the appreciation Robert developed for the man himself, beginning to see elements of his own personality in the character. 'I wasn't even really that big a fan of Dali's art,' he said. 'And even now, I kind of love the guy as a person. I mean, I find him fascinating, and in a really weird way I related to him a lot. And I appreciate his art a lot more, as with a lot of artists who are painters and stuff, I enjoy their art more once I know the sort of backstory behind it. I don't know why, really.' Robert succeeded commendably in the challenge of becoming Salvador Dali. Shortly after its release, the *Washington Times* said Robert Pattinson 'has taken on a much bigger challenge than playing a vampire – bringing a legend to life. He does an admirable job playing one of the strangest and most imaginative men to walk the earth. He's shy and trembling when he arrives at the dorm, bombastic and determined when he leaves it. The transformation is striking.'

As a small production, *Little Ashes* featured a mostly Spanish cast, aside from the inclusion of one other British actor, the up-and-coming Matthew McNulty (fresh from his appearance in Anton Corbijn's acclaimed Joy Division biopic *Control*). McNulty, who played the role of filmmaker Luis Buñuel, remembers Rob as a talented, personable actor on the verge of international stardom. 'There's something that draws you to Rob,' McNulty said. 'He is really intelligent and he's a charming chap as well. When the *Twilight* thing exploded I wasn't surprised. *Little Ashes* will be seen by a lot more people now. Previously he was just that guy from *Harry Potter*. The fact that he's playing Dali will wash that off a bit and people will see him as a proper actor.'

Much of the later interest in *Little Ashes* would be fueled by Robert's appearance in *Twilight* and his rise in popularity. 'It was a very small film,' Robert said, 'but the more I read about him, the more I liked him. I wasn't really a fan of Dali before, but I tried, I worked harder than I've worked on anything for that because playing a real person it's like, you don't want to insult them, I guess . . . It's so different playing a real person than playing someone else. It made me learn a lot about how to research and look deeper into scripts 'cause it was such a complicated character, but I was really glad I did it.'

Little Ashes stands as a turning point in Robert Pattinson's career. Not only was he now adamant about remaining an actor, but he had also succeeded in finding a challenging and important role that did not typecast him in any way. In keeping with his plan since 2006, he had found yet another uniquely challenging role that appealed to him, and circumvented the easy path to Hollywood fame and fortune. 'I didn't want to get stuck in pretty, public-school roles, or I knew I'd end up as some sort of caricature,' he said. 'Playing Dali has been a complete turning point for me. It's the first part I've had that has required really serious thought. I became completely obsessed with Dali during the filming. He was the most bizarre, complex man, but in the end I felt I could relate to him. He was basically incredibly shy.'

Although *Little Ashes* was completed well before Robert's appearance in *Twilight*, Carlo Dusi and other producers recognized an opportunity to take advantage of Pattinson's rising star by delaying the film's release in the UK and USA until 2009. However, *Little Ashes* did appear at the Raindance Film Festival in October 2008, and was also screened at the Valladolid Film Festival in Spain that same month. The film and Robert's performance received mixed reviews. Roger Ebert of the *Chicago Sun-Times* wrote, '*Little Ashes* is absorbing but not compelling. Most of its action is inward.' Of Pattinson he wrote: 'the twenty-three-year-old British star of *Twilight* (which was shot after this film). He is the heartthrob of the teenage vampire fans of *Twilight*, but here shows an admirable willingness to take on a challenging role in direct contrast to the famous Edward Cullen. Is it too much to hope that *Twilight* fans will be drawn to the work of Garcia Lorca and Buñuel? They'd be on the fast track to cultural literacy.' Steven Farber of the *Hollywood Reporter* wrote, '*Ashes* makes no claims to be an entirely accurate biopic; it's a speculative, impressionistic portrait without a lot of dramatic force or psychological depth. But it's an elegantly designed film that fascinates as often as it frustrates.' Michael O'Sullivan of the *Washington Post* stated that Pattinson failed to capture the real intensity of the Dali character, 'Beltran, for his part, makes a solidly believable Garcia Lorca. The problem is with the man with whom he's obsessed. In Pattinson's performance, we never see what Garcia Lorca sees in Dali.'

Despite the mixed reviews, the film clearly showed that Robert Pattinson had pulled away from big-budget Hollywood and established himself as a young icon in successful indie films. But within just a few months he would receive a phone call from his agent that would change his life. Stephanie Ritz had found a script that might interest him and was pushing his name forward among 5,000 other applicants for the film's lead role. Based on a string of bestselling novels by author Stephenie Meyer, the story told of a clumsy teenage girl and her love for a mysterious vampire named Edward Cullen. When Robert initially heard about the role, his first question was natural enough. To better understand the demands of the prospective part, he needed to know – along with the book's love-struck heroine Bella Swan – 'Just who is Edward Cullen?'

2

Chicago Cullen

'It's Edward who forced me to write. He's a gift of my subconscious.
I had a dream that I put on paper when I woke up. Edward was in it.
I did not need to invent him, I knew him.'
– Stephenie Meyer

Edward Anthony Masen Jr was born in Chicago, Illinois on 20 June 1901, the only son of Edward and Elizabeth Masen. Though left with precious few recollections of his mortal lifetime, Edward still remembers how he was raised – part of a traditional, moderately wealthy family in the early 20th-century, with all the benefits of his father's successful law trade. Few details are known of his education and early development, yet he was clearly eager for his chance to see the world and to serve his country. As World War One raged across the ocean, the nationalistic youth voiced his desire to enlist in the army, knowing the draft age had been lowered to eighteen in August 1918. However, his fortunes took a tragic turn in September of that year when both of his parents contracted the Spanish Influenza. His father, Edward Sr, died in the first wave of the pandemic. Soon, the mysterious vampire Doctor Carlisle Cullen came to care for his ailing mother. It was later revealed in Stephenie Meyer's second novel, *New Moon*, that Edward's mother begged the doctor with her final breaths to save her son's life by any means possible, taking action to save him in ways that no other physician could. Whether she'd guessed Carlisle's dark secret remains a mystery. But, Elizabeth's dying plea proved more than the vampire doctor could ignore. Realizing Edward was in his final days, Carlisle made up his mind to act upon her last wish, carrying the unconscious teenager to his home, leaning across the death bed, and biting Edward's neck; thus transforming him into a tragic and tormented vampire plagued by the curse of eternal life.

Thus unfolds the story of Edward's mortal life, as written by creator and author Stephenie Meyer. Prior to the storyline of *Twilight*, the chronology of the Cullen brood and Edward's lonely existence is well-documented throughout Meyer's four novels and the unpublished, yet publicly available, draft of *Midnight Sun*, a revisionist account of *Twilight* told from Edward's perspective. As the tale continues, Edward does not adapt to Carlisle Cullen's rules immediately, choosing to rebel against his adopted father. In 1927, Edward absconds from his home, leaving behind Carlisle and his adoptive mother, Esme; not to return until 1931. 'Edward obviously didn't want to become a vampire,' Robert Pattinson explains. 'He was turned into a vampire when he was unconscious, and woke up in this sort of purgatory state which he doesn't appreciate. And someone who you don't know has just put you in a situation which is difficult to understand. If someone just gives you eternal life when you've already accepted that you're dead and also that you have to kill people, you're going to have to live with that.'

Capitalizing on his newly bestowed power to read minds, Edward chose to attack society's most evil citizenry during his personal exile, hunting only the most corrupt prey to satisfy his bloodlust. However, he later shunned his evil ways, saying that the guilt weighed too heavily on his conscience, however much his victims deserved to die. He soon returned home – where Carlisle welcomed him back with open arms – determined to satisfy his urges on the blood of animals alone. In short, he became a 'vegetarian', as Edward later explains to Bella.

Around 1936, Edward and his adopted family relocate to Forks, Washington, where they first encounter the Quileute Indians, a mystical native tribe whose members have the ability to transform into werewolves. Both parties soon arrange a treaty stating that, so long as the vampires refrain from attacking humans and trespassing on Quileute land, there will be peace between the wolf pack and the Cullen coven. The Cullens remain in Forks for a few years before moving around the country, the children collecting high-school diplomas and graduation tacks, while the parents establish themselves as the most respected members of each different community they inhabit.

Over the eighty years leading up to the central plot of *Twilight*, Doctor Carlisle expanded his coven by creating additional vampires, saving several humans from a string of particularly cruel, untimely ends. Carlisle would first save Esme, a distraught, grieving mother who had recently lost her child and was abused by her husband. She became Carlisle's wife and Edward's adopted mother. Carlisle then transformed Rosalie Hale, a beautiful debutante molested by her drunken fiancé and left for dead on the city streets, as Edward's mate. However, a loving bond failed to form between Edward and Rosalie, making her nothing more than a sister to Carlisle's adopted son. Before long, Rosalie found Emmett Cullen all but mauled to death by a mountain bear. She carried him more than 100 miles to Carlisle, who in turn transformed Emmett; he became Edward's adopted brother and Rosalie's mate. Rounding out Carlisle's brood were Jasper Hale and Alice Cullen, both in search of a future after escaping calamity in their former lives. Tragically, the odd-numbered coven left the forever seventeen-year-old Edward without a mate. 'I hadn't read the books before so it's not like I had an opinion,' Robert Pattinson said of the character. 'I had to formulate my own opinion of who the guy is anyway. It's all from Bella's perspective, and she's obsessively in love in with him. She ignores all of his flaws. Stephenie Meyer gave me a manuscript of *Midnight Sun*, which is *Twilight* from Edward's perspective. And he just sees himself as the biggest moron and just disgustingly selfish. He's just a guy who is incredibly frustrated.'

At six-foot-two-inches tall, Edward Cullen stands with a svelte and muscular teenage physique, though he is technically more than 100 years old. Frustrated by heart-wrenching solitude, Edward rotates from school to school (even completing medical school twice); a popular and striking socialite understood by no one outside his close-knit coven, he painstakingly maintains his distance from the rest of the world. From the opening passages of *Twilight* on, Edward is constantly described as an extremely gorgeous being, with Bella repeatedly comparing him to the mythical Greek god Adonis, his marble skin icy to the touch and extraordinarily pale. His facial features are angular and perfect, with high cheekbones, a chiseled jaw line and full lips that leave Miss Swan mesmerized. His tousled dark hair shimmers an atypical bronze shade, which he inherited from his biological mother. His eyes are topaz, and when he goes a significant period of time without feeding, his appearance changes that much more drastically: his eyes darken to pitch black, and purple bruise-like shadows stretch beneath them. As revealed in *Midnight Sun*, after years of sitting among generations of oblivious high-school students, he is further taken with Bella, as she is the only mortal to observe that his eyes change color.

Meyer's creation of Edward and the Cullen brood is a revisionist account of traditional vampire lore. After centuries of literary and cinematic tales of cryptic vampire figures, gone are the caskets, garlic, Transylvanian castles and midnight-colored capes. Robert Pattinson himself was pleased by Meyer's new account and avoidance of typical vampire clichés. 'Luckily, Stephenie didn't have vampire lore in the book,' he said. 'It's very specific, and the characters in the book even kind of joke about the mythology about vampires, and so you can kind of get another element of realism there.' The

Cullen brood are a cultured family of socialites who walk among mortals, popular and well-respected in the tight-knit Forks community. Meyer's vampires avoid sunlight not because it will kill them, but rather because it reveals their magnificent beauty to humans. Though he is embarrassed and sickened by his image and existence, Edward's skin sparkles like diamonds when he willingly reveals himself to Bella for the first time.

Like other members of the Cullen coven in the *Twilight* series, Edward possesses more than just incredible beauty and refined style. Bella describes the unearthly beauty of each family member, but Edward is the fastest by far, showing Bella his incredible speed as he runs up mountains and trees. Although he is not the strongest in his coven, he is one of the best fighters (along with Jasper), increasing his desire to protect his love and his family. Edward never sleeps and explains that, like other vampires, he does not need to breathe, choosing to do so out of habit alone. Central to the book – and his interaction with Bella – is Edward's ability to hear the thoughts of everyone around him, although he finds himself incredibly frustrated by his inability to tap into Bella's thoughts.

After all, as Edward explains in *Midnight Sun*, his interest in Forks High's newest student is more than just idle curiosity. Enabling him to stay one step ahead of the humans around them, the Cullens have come to depend on Edward's gift to keep them safe. Edward and his dazzlingly beautiful siblings could never pass through the world unnoticed. The subject of whisperings in the cafeteria and endless speculation, they're accustomed to the attention. Yet there's always the danger that someone might see through their spellbinding mystique. Inspired by film, literature and folklore, someone could potentially guess correctly. Could curious newcomer Bella Swan be the next mortal to uncover their secret? Thus begins Edward's fascination with her . . .

Every publisher and literary agent dreams of a client like Stephenie Meyer. The success of the *Twilight* books had only been rivaled by Britain's J.K. Rowling with the *Harry Potter* series. But Meyer's stories, telling of the forbidden love between a vampire and mortal, sold more than twenty-two million copies in 2008 alone. *Twilight* was the bestselling book of the year, and by late 2008, when the first part of the film series would finally hit the big screen, the tale of the teen affair had sold more than forty-two million copies in thirty-seven languages worldwide. Stephenie Meyer's inspiration is well documented and can be recited by heart by every loyal fan of the series. On 2 June 2003 the author had a dream in which a vampire fell in love with a young girl, but at the same time had a powerful thirst for her blood. 'I already knew he was a vampire and he was sparkly and beautiful and she was just kind of ordinary and in awe of this creature,' Meyer said. 'He was explaining how hard it was not to kill her and she was amazed that he wanted to be around her even if it was risking her life.' The dream vision of Edward was so vivid that she sat down and wrote what would become chapter thirteen of the first novel, even though she had never published a book in her life.

Meyer's extraordinary accomplishment paralleled many of the same struggles of *Harry Potter* author Rowling a decade prior. Once she completed the novel, it was rejected by agents and publishers fourteen times. A teetotal practicing Mormon, Meyer's faith played a very important role in the development of Edward's character. 'We have free will,' Meyer said, referring to it as a 'gift from God'. 'If you tie that up with something like, I don't know, cocaine, then you don't really have a lot of freedom anymore.' This sentiment parallels the Cullen brood's predicament. While they fervently desire human blood, they have made a moral choice to abstain from it, and sate their hunger on the blood of animals.

The fact that she's been an avid reader her entire life may have been another contributing factor to Meyer's ability to churn out the massive draft that would become *Twilight*. As a reader, she'd at least learned to grasp the depth of particular characters, how they interacted, how dialogue was written properly and how to bring a plot from beginning to end. 'Growing up I was an avid reader – the thicker the book, the better,' said Meyer. Her notable favorites – *Pride and Prejudice, Gone with the Wind, The Sword of Shannara, Jane Eyre* and *Rebecca* – are all lengthy novels with well-developed and complicated characters. 'I'm a huge fan of Orson Scott Card, and Jane Austen – I can't go through a year without re-reading her stuff again.'

In fact, it was Jane Austen's early 19th-century writing that influenced the name of the vampire who would soon bury himself in the heart of every *Twilight* fan worldwide. When creating the character, Stephenie Meyer said that she wanted to choose a name that captured the romantic nature of this damned beast. Yet Meyer's challenge really centered on avoiding traditional 20th- and even 21st-century names that might invite comparison with today's modern literary or film heroes. Drawing inspiration from classic romance tales, Meyer sought a name that 'had once been considered romantic, but had fallen out of popularity for decades'. She had little problem choosing the name Edward, inspired by the brooding employer Mr Edward Rochester in Charlotte Brontë's

1847 novel *Jane Eyre*, and the charmingly reserved Edward Ferrars in Jane Austen's first novel *Sense and Sensibility*. From Old English, the name Edward literally means 'rich protector' or 'wealthy guardian'. Meyer found that the name fit well; perfectly characterizing the young vampire and referencing his natural urge to protect his love Bella. The Gaelic root word 'Evart' also denotes a substance with sparkling qualities, something that defined Edward's skin and appearance when exposed to sunlight.

At the beginning of *Twilight*, Edward's tragedy is shown in his splintering teenage solitude, a school boy searching for a connection that never reveals itself through decades of new towns, new schools, and new classmates. When his family finally returns to Forks, a combination of fear, lust and protective instincts overwhelm him when a new girl moves to his town. Manically depressed and silently tortured, Edward himself finally understands what it is that has been missing from his existence. When Isabella Swan arrives to live with her father, he catches her scent and tries to read her thoughts. Unable to penetrate her mind, he listens to the thoughts of the other students to learn what he can about her, only to realize that all of the other male students are greatly interested in her. In *Midnight Sun*, he states that she has the sweetest blood he has smelled in more than eighty years. Consumed by a protective urge, he soon finds himself conflicted, the power of her scent and desire to kill her overwhelming his thoughts. When Bella is forced to partner with him in biology, Edward smells her blood, desires to kill her and considers murdering the entire class to get to her. He fantasizes about how he would go about killing each member of the class before finally reaching her, hinting that he does not want to provide any time for her blood to cool. After storming out of the lab and failing to transfer to another class, Edward casts himself into exile for one week, traveling to Denali to stay with another 'vegetarian' coven in an attempt to quell his urges.

'He's spent his entire life repressing everything,' said Robert Pattinson of his character. 'He's kind of ashamed of himself when he lets his facade of formality break. When Bella comes into his life. He doesn't want to feel anything. He wants to make his world smaller and smaller because he doesn't feel like he belongs in it. He either wants to be a human or die because his existence is completely pointless. That's why he doesn't talk to anyone. He doesn't really feel anything in the book apart from when Bella comes. He's literally counting the cracks in the wall and stuff. Every single day is exactly the same thing. If he feels anything he shuts it down immediately.'

Upon his return, he finally introduces himself to Bella, but remains frustrated by his inability to read her thoughts and his constant desire to taste her blood. After saving her from a runaway van, he tries to convince her that she is imagining his incredible speed and impossible strength. While she is unable to shake her curiosity, Edward withdraws from her again, refusing to speak to her for a time. But he soon grows jealous of the other male students when he reads their thoughts, particularly Mike Newton, who has decided that he is going to try to ask Bella out. Edward responds by sneaking into Bella's room late in the evening to watch her sleep. When she calls his name in the depths of her slumber, Edward realizes that he has fallen in love. Over the next few weeks, he begins to follow and protect her, and after one night together in Port Angeles, he discovers that she knows what he is and that she has fallen in love with him too. A passionate confession follows. Edward tells her that for almost ninety years he has drifted through the world, yearning for something more and fated not to find it – until Bella Swan was born.

'*Twilight* taps into that young girl's primacy of first love and forbidden love, and how much more forbidden is it than to fall in love with a vampire?' asks Karen Rosenfelt, *Twilight*'s executive producer. 'Bella herself is accessible to girls. Bella captures the side we all have, that feeling of being an outsider looking in while still trying to keep our iconoclastic nature.' Despite the love growing between them, Edward still warns Bella of his bloodlust and the danger she faces by staying with him.

'The relationship between the characters is kind of like Edward goes, "Every day, I really want to kill you, you don't understand," and Bella goes, "I don't care, I love you!"' Robert said. 'I guess the whole thing is that you can only have that kind of love story when you're young and you're sort of overcome by your emotions and it seems so life-or-death.' The complication of a vampire falling in love with a human creates a remarkable amount of concern and tension within the Cullen brood. Any knowledge of their existence threatens the family, while Bella is placing herself in a remarkable amount of danger by being in the presence of lustful beings who are partially driven to kill her and drink her blood. Bella, consumed by love, accepts the risk and is soon invited to Edward's house to meet his family. With the exception of Rosalie, the Cullens immediately like her and feel a need to protect Bella given Edward's noticeable transformation since falling in love with her.

Alice Cullen soon invites the couple to play a game of baseball. But as Bella watches the Cullens play the sport during a lightning storm, several unexpected vampire guests arrive: James, Laurent, and Victoria. James, a tracker, catches Bella's scent, contemplates her as his next meal and decides to hunt Bella for sport. After taking advice from Bella, Alice, and Emmett, Edward allows them to try using Bella's plan: Bella convinces her father Charlie that she is leaving town, and Alice and Jasper take her to hide in Phoenix. Edward tries to lead James away, but loses his trail. He then flies to Phoenix to see Bella and finds James, who has mortally wounded Bella and bitten her hand. Edward first thinks that Bella is dead and goes crazy with pain and guilt. He is described by Bella as an angel, sobbing tearlessly, but this makes him appear more beautiful than she ever has seen him. Edward's family arrives and destroys James, while Edward sucks the venom out of Bella's system to prevent her from becoming a vampire herself. He then lifts her up and walks her out of the burning building. After they return to Forks, Edward takes Bella to their prom. Much to her dismay, he resolves that he isn't going to change her into a vampire, but she is adamant that the discussion isn't over.

Edward Cullen quickly became one of the most iconic male characters in vampire history. As more than forty-two million copies of his story swept off of bookshelves, what every reader wanted to know was: when would this book be adapted into a movie, and which young actor would fill the role of the dreamy vampire?

8

the Search for Edward Cullen

'I'd seen a zillion really cute guys. But that was the problem. They all looked like
the super-cute kid in your high school. The prom king or the captain of the football
team. They didn't look like they were from another world and time.'
– Catherine Hardwicke

Following a major bidding war, MTV Films and Maverick Films announced on 11 March 2004 that they had acquired the production rights to a high-school vampire novel centered on a girl named Bella Swan. Before long, the shy but spirited teenager falls in love with a pale, mysterious classmate, who seems determined to push her away. According to the script summary, 'The new couple leads a rival vampire clan to pursue them and attempt to force her to decide if she, too, wishes to become one of the undead.' With Paramount Pictures set to distribute the film, Stephenie Meyer's creation would begin pre-production one full year before the first book was even published. For Mcyer, as for any writer who has ever put pen to paper, a near impossible dream was unfolding.

However, shortly after the contracted screenwriters assumed control of Meyer's creation, they quickly deviated from the authentic storyline tailored by the Mormon writer. MTV developed a script that bore very little resemblance to Meyer's epic (save the character names and the fact that vampires were part of the storyline). The absurd script featured night-vision goggles and long fangs, and had transformed clumsy Bella into a popular high-school track star, perhaps trying to add a potential plot device directed at Edward Cullen's remarkable speed. 'They could have put that movie out, called it something else, and no one would have known it was *Twilight*,' author Meyer said of the new script. Luckily for the legions of fans who had memorized passages and fallen in love with the residents of Forks, Paramount put the project on hold. Whether track-star Bella and lightning-fast Edward were slated to have a foot race up above the cloud break (rather than a piggyback ride), *Twilight* fans will never know.

It took another three years before Summit Entertainment, having recently reinvented itself as a full-service film studio, considered redevelopment of the MTV adaptation. Erik Feig, the production president of Summit, would first need to orchestrate a deal with Meyer, who'd been disillusioned by the original MTV version. Feig guaranteed that the film would stay true to Meyer's vision of the characters (removing the night goggles and track-star persona), with a promise that 'no vampire character will be depicted with canine or incisor teeth longer or more pronounced than may be found in human beings'. Stephenie Meyer enthusiastically accepted, soon announcing on her website that *Twilight* would become a major motion picture. 'I am very excited to announce that *Twilight* has been optioned by Summit Entertainment,' she wrote on her blog. 'I have been negotiating with Summit on a great contract that I think will really protect the story. The people at Summit seem quite enthusiastic about doing *Twilight* the right way, and I'm looking forward to working with them.'

The *Twilight* novel naturally lent itself to film adaptation, with its vivid descriptions of Forks' scenic landscape, capricious weather patterns, and small-town charm. But set choices and on-location decisions were of little concern to Meyer's hardcore faithful. Those issues were to be left to the set directors. All anyone who had ever read *Twilight* really wanted to know was: who would portray the striking residents of Forks, most importantly Edward Cullen? Five thousand male actors sent their résumés, clips, and headshots in the hope of winning the role of a lifetime, and many received casting calls for their shot at portraying Meyer's reinvention of vampire lore. The team to choose from this staggering list of contenders included Stephenie Meyer and the recently announced director, Catherine Hardwicke. Buried in the book of thousands of headshots and professional bios, Edward Cullen waited.

Rarely do cast searches for fictional characters reach any further than the back pages of Hollywood gossip magazines. But Edward Cullen was no ordinary part. Neither was Bella, Jacob Black, nor any other member of the Cullen coven. It was predicted from the outset that whoever won the role of Edward would become an international superstar, and the overwhelming pressure to find the right actor started with Stephenie Meyer herself. Shortly after the new script came under screenwriter Melissa Rosenberg's command, Stephenie wrote that her first choice for the role of Edward was Henry Cavill, a cleft-jawed British actor who had recently caught the attention of casting directors following his role as Stephen Colley in *I Capture the Castle*, an adaptation of a Dodie Smith novel.

'The only actor I've ever seen who I think could come close to pulling off Edward Cullen is Henry Cavill,' Meyer wrote on her blog. However,

Cavill had recently turned twenty-four years old, and it was clear that he would not be able to successfully portray an eternal seventeen-year-old, especially if the film series spanned several additional movies. (On her blog, Meyer even called for a moment of silence when she admitted that too much time had passed since the story was first optioned and that Cavill was now too old to play the part.) Since Bella Swan describes Edward's face as one of near-impossible, airbrushed-model perfection, casting the role was going to be a daunting task for everyone involved, especially given the public's somewhat intrusive demands. 'We needed someone who was both pretty and scary,' Meyer said. 'The one guy that kids were always saying they wanted for Edward was Tom Welling from *Smallville*. He's beautiful! But could you ever imagine being afraid of him? We did not have a good option until Rob came along.'

'Everybody has such an idealized vision of Edward,' *Twilight* director Catherine Hardwicke said about fans of the franchise. 'They were rabid [about who I was going to cast]. Like, old ladies saying, "You better get it right."' Though Logan Lerman and Tyler Posey had been early suggestions for Jacob, and Rachel McAdams and Emily Browning for the part of Bella, the online blog and message-board speculation truly centered on the production's search for Edward Cullen. Early candidates for the role included Orlando Bloom, Chace Crawford, Hayden Christensen, Gerard Way, and Tom Sturridge, a long-time friend of Robert Pattinson's who had worked with him on *Vanity Fair* and in the Barnes Theater Group. On Stephenie Meyer's website, Hayden Christensen quickly became the most popular choice. 'We definitely checked out all the fan suggestions to see if they were still the right age, or if they were good, or available, or on another show or something. But none of them really worked out,' Hardwicke said.

Stipulations for who would play Edward would have to be put in place in order to find the actor able to portray the most attractive and seductive vampire in the history of literature and film. While arguments regarding vampire films and television shows past had placed Brad Pitt and David Boreanaz in the top tier of the most physically beautiful on-screen vampires of all time, the production team needed someone who could surpass them both and bring Edward's remarkable beauty, tormented love and lust, and protective intimacy to the screen. That actor needed to be fewer than twenty-one years of age and couldn't be a model, a singer, or member of a band. It also seemed well understood that the winner of the role would immediately move to the A-list of Hollywood players, so it was important to find someone who could handle the pressure of the role and the immense physical and emotional toll of skyrocketing popularity from day one. Bill George, who coordinated the special effects for the film, recalled that Hardwicke provided a few additional requirements for Edward Cullen. In early concept artwork depicting a long-haired Edward, the director repeatedly spoke about to the character's 'inherent darkness'. 'Catherine described the character as darkly masculine,' George said. 'She said if this movie was made thirty years ago, Edward wouldn't be a vampire, but a biker, that Bella would be falling in love with a biker from the wrong side of the tracks.'

But above all else, the role demanded that both Bella and Edward have an on-screen chemistry that was honest and parallel to the steamy interactions portrayed in Meyer's novels. Once the chemistry was found, the production team felt that filming would take care of itself. Of course, that failed to address the concerns of the global fan base that was already debating the ideal cast on blogs and message boards all around the world. As casting progressed, Robert Pattinson certainly didn't seem to be among the early favorites. And more importantly, it was unclear if he would be able to handle the role's immense challenges as previously outlined by the major decision makers.

In the fall of 2007, Robert was living in London with a friend, clearly becoming weary of the idea of being an actor. Still playing music in small clubs, he had made it abundantly clear to his agents that he was in the process of taking time out. 'I was living in London and I was a bit jaded with acting, to be honest,' Robert said. 'I was doing music in London. I wasn't even really thinking about acting. I really liked my American agent here though, and she said, "Listen, you haven't been here all year, you've got to come and do some casting auditions."'

Though he enjoyed living in Soho – finding he was still able to quietly blend into his favorite city – he did begin to feel that he owed it to himself and others around him to spend some time in search of film and television work. *Twilight* was among a number of potential auditions awaiting him in the United States. Still, there were growing concerns for Pattinson regarding his available opportunities. Few producers in Los Angeles, if any, really knew of him or remembered him from his previous work. Though Hardwicke had seen a picture of Robert Pattinson and knew his work from *Harry Potter and the Goblet of Fire*, she appeared underwhelmed at first. In addition, his struggles with an American accent and limited résumé challenged his potential worldwide appeal. Still, Robert's agent pushed his name forward, and pretty soon he had entered the blogosphere as a potential candidate. However, just as he had been in the early stages of casting and headshot selection, Robert Pattinson remained, in the words of *Twilight* producer Greg Mooradian, 'more of a dark horse'.

The next problem was that Robert knew little of the backstory regarding *Twilight*, or whether or not the series had any real potential for longevity. The reality was that Pattinson simply saw Edward Cullen as another film job with indie appeal, one that might offer him some opportunity to reignite his recently lackluster career. Still, even though it was just another job to him, he was thinking long term, and wanted to do all that he could to avoid making a cheap teen film, ever conscious that the wrong choice – should it be panned by critics and shunned by mass audiences – could potentially destroy his career. 'I didn't want to do a stupid teen movie,' Robert said. 'Even little kids don't want to hear you say the same pat stuff, it's boring! I'm thinking about my career in the long term, rather than just trying to milk one thing for whatever it's worth. I specifically hadn't done anything which anyone would see since *Harry Potter*, because I wanted to teach myself how to act. I didn't want to be an idiot. *Twilight* came kind of randomly, and I didn't really know what it was when it first started. I wanted to do two or three more little things and then do something bigger, and then this kind of happened and I was like, "Well, okay."'

When his agent Stephanie Ritz called to say that Catherine Hardwicke wanted him to read for the part of Edward, he was, at the time, totally unaware of the growing literary phenomenon. He also didn't know that from the moment Meyer had announced that the book would be adapted for the screen, thousands upon thousands of fans had been posting heart-felt opinions about him and every other prospective Edward Cullen. All he really knew was that he needed to get his acting career back on track. Perhaps if Robert had known the unique demands of the role and the level of fame it would surely bring him, he may have reconsidered. 'I was living in England and it wasn't big there,' he said of Meyer's novel. 'I actually tried to read it five months before when somebody had told me about it, and I read a few pages, and I thought, "Oh, this isn't my thing." And I didn't know that there was a phenomenon. I thought it was a little bit "girly". But then I read the script and it cut out a lot of the descriptions . . . It read more like an action script. So later, I went back to the book and saw what the differences had been. I looked at it a bit more objectively. I liked the book better when I came back to it the second time.'

But as soon as Robert began to re-immerse himself in the *Twilight* series, he realized the most glaringly obvious problem for anyone trying to portray Edward. Robert didn't consider himself qualified for the part given the character's extraordinary physical and emotional appeal. 'I read the first fifty pages, up until when he gets introduced, and I was just like, "No." Because I was really fat [at the time I read it]. So it was just embarrassing. I thought the whole thing was embarrassing, even turning up to the audition. I hadn't read the whole book before the audition, but even [from] the four-line synopsis – "Edward is the perfect being. He's so witty and beautiful. He's crazy and funny. He'll open doors for you. He'll drive you in his Volvo" – I thought even turning up would be embarrassing.'

Feeling less than optimistic about how he'd measure up to the demands of playing this flawless being, Robert made his doubts known to Stephanie Ritz. 'When I was reading the script I remember telling my agent, "I can't do this. It's physically impossible to do this." The character has these amazing physical qualities that are impossible to have: he has a great body, he's gorgeous.'

The first major character to be cast in *Twilight* was Kristen Stewart as the heroine, Bella. Stewart made a name for herself playing Jodie Foster's daughter in *Panic Room*, and Tracy Tatro in Sean Penn's *Into the Wild*. 'We first had Kristen, because I fell madly in love with her in *Into the Wild*,' Hardwicke said. 'I thought she was amazing and so expressive of that longing and that desire. So we had Kristen, and then we kind of narrowed the guys down to like our semi-finals.'

Indeed, Hardwicke was down to her final four actors. She would eventually reveal that each of her 'semi-finalists' were called for private auditions on the same day at her house in Venice, California. Speaking at a fan convention in Arizona in August 2009, Hardwicke named Jackson Rathbone, Ben Barnes (who starred in *Easy Virtue* with Jessica Biel), and Shiloh Fernandez (who starred in *Cadillac Records*) as the other young actors who had reached the final four. (Jackson eventually won the part of Edward's brother, Jasper Hale.) Hardwicke apparently referred to the contenders as, 'Bachelor one, two, three and four.' Pattinson flew to Venice for his private audition at Hardwicke's home. By then, the tired director had already screened hundreds of potential Edwards and was growing increasingly frustrated with the casting process. 'I'd seen a zillion really cute guys,' Hardwicke said. 'But that was the problem. They all looked like the super-cute kid in your high school. The prom king or the captain of the football team. They didn't look like they were from another world and time.'

Previous page: *Robert's unique sense of style,*
chiseled features and soft British accent inspired
People *magazine to add the young actor to its 2008*
list of the Sexiest Men Alive.

Above: *Edward in the sunlight: A bearded*
Rob takes time out to pose for pictures at the
Rome International Film Festival, October 2008.

Opposite: *Classic charm: Rob and Kristen pose*
at the Rome International Film Festival,
October 2008.

Overleaf: *Robert Pattinson, Kristen Stewart and*
Taylor Lautner pose as their Twilight *characters*
during an Entertainment Weekly *cover shoot used*
to promote the film in July 2008.

Above left: *Where the hysteria began . . .
Rob Pattinson and Kristen Stewart pause on
the red carpet at* Twilight's *world premiere in
Woodward, California, November 2008.*

Above right: *Having just accepted the award
for Best Kiss at the 2009 MTV Movie Awards,
Rob and Kristen move tantalizingly closer.*

Opposite: *The road to success: Robert gets a
taste of things to come on the red carpet before a
screening of* Twilight *at the Rome International
Film Festival, October 2008.*

Overleaf: *The eyebrows have it: Robert attends
a photo-call in Paris while promoting* Twilight,
December 2008.

He'd barely set foot in the house and been introduced to Kristen Stewart when, without further ado, Rob was informed that he'd have to read three scenes while Hardwicke taped his interactions with the actress. Having already read with and kissed three other actors that day, '[Kristen] was kind of sleepy and just hanging out – and then Robert appeared in the room,' Hardwicke said. 'His hair was a little different – it was his Dali hair, with the black bangs.' They began his audition with a reading of the biology class scene in Hardwicke's kitchen, before moving outside to read the meadow scene.

His nerves rattled and his uncertainty mounting, Robert admits he relied on pills to relax for the audition. 'I took half a Valium and then went into this thing – and all this stuff happened. It was the first time I've ever taken Valium,' he said, before realizing that admissions of prescription drug use might be frowned upon by some individuals, and adding: 'A quarter. A quarter of a Valium. I tried to do it for another audition, and it just completely backfired – I was passing out.'

After completing the two scenes and thinking that he was nearly done for the day, the director and Stewart surprised him with the context of the third audition scenario. Hardwicke called for Stewart and Pattinson to conduct a love scene in the director's own bed while she again filmed the interaction. 'Kristen already had to kiss three other guys that day,' Hardwicke said. Then it came time for the young actor they were referring to as 'Bachelor number four'.

With the director filming test footage to show the studio, the Valium clearly wasn't settling Robert's anxiety. 'He was a bit nervous, because suddenly you've just met a girl and you're going to start making out with the person – and someone is filming,' said Hardwicke. '[Pattinson] was really wild on the first take – use your imagination. I had to tell him, "This is going to be a PG-13 movie!" and have him settle down a little bit.'

Robert has repeatedly commented that Kristen's calmness helped him relax and ease into the steamy audition. 'It was funny. When I got into bed with Kristen I said, "I've only known you for an hour and we are in bed." I think I must have gone way over the top with it as well, because I remember looking up afterwards and Catherine Hardwicke had a look on her face as if to say, "What are you doing? You look like you're having a seizure!"'

But Robert hadn't taken it too far. In fact, Hardwicke was immensely impressed with how quickly the chemistry between Stewart and Pattinson developed in the bedroom. 'It was electric,' Hardwicke said. 'The room shorted out, the sky opened up, and I was like, "This is going to be good."'

Robert, of course, had mixed feelings. 'I thought they were going to say to me, "No, thank you. Next." Honestly, I went to the audition without preparing. I didn't know the lines or anything and Kristen was there. I didn't know she was going to be Bella. I was frantically nervous and Kristen was very strong and calm.'

But Kristen Stewart disagreed, describing the pain of Robert's interpretation of the eternally teenaged vampire as an element that increased their chemistry. 'Not to put down any of the other actors who came in,' Stewart said, 'because they were really good, but everyone came in playing Edward as this perfect, happy-go-lucky guy, but I got hardcore pain from Rob. It was purely just connection.'

Hardwicke took twenty-four hours to make a decision on Pattinson. At this stage, there was clearly no need for haste. After seeing hundreds of potentials and wheedling the list down to a final select few, she was willing to wait just a few more hours before relaying her decision to the producers. 'No matter how much I fall in love with the person, I make myself review the tape, to make sure I wasn't just overwhelmed by something in the air,' Hardwicke said.

Stewart, on the other hand, had already made up her mind, lobbying to Hardwicke shortly after Robert walked out the door. 'I knew in the audition that he was sort of the only guy I could really work with,' said Stewart. 'Everybody came in doing something empty and shallow and thoughtless. I know that's a great thing to say about all the other actors – but Rob understood that it wasn't a frivolous role.'

Robert left the audition as uncertain about his potential as when he walked in the door. He'd traveled across the United States for a part for which he felt he wasn't even qualified. Still, he walked away feeling that the chemistry between Edward and Bella had been sparked during his audition read-throughs of the meadow and bedroom scenes. 'I went in having no idea how to play the part at all and thinking there was no chance of getting it,' said Robert. 'I mean, Catherine literally didn't say anything during the whole audition. She just filmed. And Kristen did it so differently to how I was expecting Bella to be played that it kind of shocked a performance out of me. And it was the first time in a long time that I'd had an organic experience in an audition. And I thought that there could be a lot of depth to the story. But I only realized in the audition.'

Hardwicke spent the rest of that day and part of the following day reviewing the tape. Describing the chemistry between Robert and Kristen as 'two magnets coming together', she finally felt satisfied – after months of searching – that she had found her Edward Cullen. 'It was a massive challenge to find Edward,' said Hardwicke. 'Not many actors can live up to the image in the book – the pale skin and the otherworldly beauty.' While most of the actors that sought the role of Edward Cullen were handsome, they all looked too much like the all-American guy. 'Pattinson was different; he had everything we needed, and he had that angular face and kind of mysterious Edward aura.'

But Hardwicke still had to convince Summit Entertainment – the studio would be risking millions of dollars to back the film – that the relatively unknown and untested Robert Pattinson could carry this production on his shoulders. She spoke with Erik Feig, who had viewed the studio test films and shared any early concerns he might have had. 'There was a call from the head of the studio,' Hardwicke said. The production unit was asking if she was absolutely sure that she could 'make this guy handsome'. The director was convinced she could. With the chemistry between the actors in place, she began to assemble her team to create an on-screen version of Edward Cullen. 'He's supposed to be the most beautiful man in the whole world. Perfectly sculpted cheekbones. Who can live up to that?' asked Hardwicke. 'Well actually, Rob Pattinson can.'

Summit Entertainment eventually agreed and formally announced on 11 December 2007 that they had cast Robert Pattinson for the part of Edward Cullen. The press release quoted Feig, who said of Robert, 'It's always a challenge to find the right actor for a part that has lived so vividly in the imaginations of readers but we took the responsibility seriously and are confident, with Rob Pattinson, that we have found the perfect Edward for our Bella in *Twilight*.'

In the age of viral communication, the news spread from London to the Far East in a matter of minutes. And not everyone was overjoyed with the studio and director's decision. 'There was a huge, universal backlash about my being cast as Edward Cullen,' said Robert. 'Seventy-five thousand *Twilight* fans signed a petition against me. But, I mean, I expected it.' Certain fans, all of whom had their own passionate preconceptions about what Edward Cullen should look like, were hastily lashing out, and some of the articles and postings were less than complimentary. 'I stopped reading after I saw the signatures saying, "Please, anyone else,"' Pattinson said, laughing. 'I was completely expecting complaints from *Twilight* fans. That's why I didn't want to play the part in the first place. Who could possibly play it apart from, like, Zac Efron?'

The bloggers questioned his résumé, his hair, his posture, his ability to utilize an American accent. Some postings even included artwork and previous screenshots from his earlier work. Lesser-known roles were coming back to haunt him, especially *Ring of the Nibelungs*. Robert's mother would read several reports that supported the 'anyone but Rob' message. She read online that her only son was 'wretched and ugly' and had 'the face of a gargoyle'.

'My mom sent me some stuff, which she thought was really funny, when I was already in America. They had this picture from this Viking film I did where I looked like someone had beaten me in the face with a frying pan. I was wearing this disgusting wig. And they were like, "This is Edward." It was a petition, which they were going to send to Summit saying, "We will not go and see the movie." It got up to 75,000 signings. This is about three days after I got cast. I was thinking, "Thanks for sending that mom!" That was my welcome into *Twilight*.'

As public sentiment continued to grow more rabidly anti-Pattinson, Robert was clearly in need of an ally, someone in his corner who could help sway fans of the *Twilight* series to back him prior to the shooting of the film. The most logical candidate, of course, was Stephenie Meyer, the creator of Edward Cullen. Meyer soon spoke with satisfaction upon hearing the news, writing on her blog, 'I am ecstatic with Summit's choice for Edward. There are very few actors who can look both dangerous and beautiful at the same time, and even fewer who I can picture in my head as Edward. Robert Pattinson is going to be amazing.'

With the author's blessing, Robert Pattinson could begin his transformation.

9

Becoming Edward Cullen

'If you really prepare for a role, there's going
to be a moment in which he's all you can think of.'
– Robert Pattinson

The *Twilight* cast had been assembled, and the script was entering its final stages of development. But before Hardwicke could begin filming with her carefully selected actors and actresses, a squad of stylists and wardrobe specialists were gathered to carefully craft the physicality of each one of Stephenie Meyer's characters. 'Wardrobe, hair, make-up – it all has to look unified or it's not going to work,' said *Twilight* hairstylist Mary Ann Valdes. 'Our three departments work closely together. Wardrobe leads the process, because hair and make-up is a little more flexible, while costumes have to be decided ahead of time and things have to be fitted. The kind of clothes being worn will also accentuate the make-up.'

Everyone involved immediately recognized the challenge that lay ahead of them. Fans of the series had already placed an incredible burden on the production team regarding its casting decisions, and the pressure to remain loyal to the author's vision and to bring the romantic beauty of Edward, Jacob and the Cullens to the big screen was only set to intensify. 'We had a lot of challenges because we have a big cast of characters, but they're all very specifically described in the book,' said Hardwicke. 'So people know what every single character is supposed to look like. And the most challenging one of course [is] Edward.'

The pressure to mold the perfect Edward Cullen would not fall on the shoulders of the actor alone. An entire team of filmmakers, designers, wardrobe experts and stylists would work together in order to create one of the most anticipated film characters in recent cinema history. Hardwicke told *Vanity Fair* magazine, '[Producers] called me up and they literally said, "Catherine, do you think you can make this guy look good?" So I said, "Here's what I'm going to do. I'm going to get his hair back to a different color, do a different style. He would work with a trainer from now on. My cinematographer is great with lighting. He will study the cheekbones, and I promise you, we'll make the guy look good."'

Given that Edward is 107 years old in the story, it can only be assumed that he has developed a well-cultured sense of style during his lifetime. His extensive collection of music – which he shares with Bella shortly after introducing her to his family – acts as a subtle reminder to readers and viewers of how he has steadily established his artistic preferences over a century on earth; therefore, the same taste needed to be visible in his clothing and appearance. In planning costumes for Edward, designer Wendy Chuck conducted an immense amount of research on period-specific fashion styles from the past two centuries. She eventually settled on the designs of the classical Edwardian era, the early 20th-century period from 1901 to 1910, shortly before Edward transformed from a mortal into a vampire. (The Edwardian era was a time of massive imbalance of wealth and power in Europe and named after the English monarch Edward VII, who ruled during this decade.) The initial production sketches featured Robert Pattinson dressed in classical jackets and tight, finely-tailored pants and suits with pronounced shirt collars. However, the vision quickly transformed into a more contemporary look, one that incorporated designer jeans and custom T-shirts. 'One of the difficulties with the Cullens was they had to blend with high-school kids,' said Wendy Chuck. 'In the book, they are described as rock-star gorgeous. They have money and wear designer clothes. And they go to school. They had to not look freakishly different. It became a lot of about the fit and the silhouette. So for example, we put Rob in well-cut jeans and T-shirts and classical lace-up boots. Things evolve as you work on a character.'

But while the wardrobe team pondered well-tailored clothing, hair designer Mary Ann Valdes was finding that Edward Cullen's hair had taken on a life of its own during pre-production. Valdes was responsible for meticulously maintaining Robert's hair during the filming, and said that she was explicitly loyal to the character's description in the novels. Early on, however, there were a number of different proposals for the color of Edward Cullen's hair, right down to the most miniscule differences between comparable shades. The hairstyle was naturally going to follow the bronze-tint, as described in the novels. Still the look could not detract from Edward's pale complexion, which would be highlighted with softer-colored make-up. 'I talked over with Catherine the different shades of bronze hair before I ever met Rob,' said Mary Ann Valdes. '[Pattinson's] normal hair is like a medium golden brown, and it had been dyed black for a previous movie. The black had faded to a dark color and two inches of his re-growth had come in and he had two tones going. We had to remove the color from a previous movie to put a new color in it.'

In pre-production, there were also conflicting opinions as to what the length of Edward Cullen's hair should be. Promotional pictures of Pattinson depicted his character with short bronze hair, and Summit Entertainment really liked the look. But Hardwicke spent an afternoon pondering what Robert might look like with hair extensions and privately instructed Valdes to implant them for studio concept photos. 'I thought it would be cool if Rob had long hair,' Hardwicke said. 'So we put extensions on Rob and he just hated it. He sat there in the chair for eight hours and was like, "No."'

It was ultimately decided by the parties involved that the hair extensions hid the upper reaches of Pattinson's distinctive jaw line and needed to be abandoned. They soon reverted to the natural, gelled look portrayed in the film, which pleased Erik Feig and the production staff. However, Valdes indicated that Hardwicke had the final say on the matter and could have overturned the decision at any time. 'If Catherine really liked the long hair, she would talk the studio into it,' Valdes said. 'The hair extensions went on that day, and we took them out the next day. We all agreed [it should be short]. But Catherine had to see for herself that the short hair was best. If she hadn't seen the longer hair, she'd still be wondering.'

There was little argument that Edward Cullen's hair was critical, not only to satisfy the production team, but also the legions of fans who had created their own intimate visions of the vampire. Nearly two years after *Twilight* became a record-breaking commercial success, Robert believes that his hair has taken on its own personality on the sets of the three *Twilight Saga* movies to have been filmed thus far. In a joint interview on the set of *Eclipse*, Pattinson attempted to explain that his hair had become 'seventy-five percent' of his performance. While he playfully claimed that during production of *Twilight* he was asked to wear hair extensions that 'fell all the way down' to his hips, Kristen Stewart appeared to have a more accurate recollection of the events. 'He doesn't remember. He's remembering how they made him feel, but they were just, like, down to here,' she said, pointing to her shoulders.

Pattinson shrugged and laughed at Stewart's comments, seeming to believe that the final say in the matter was his. 'So I told them, "Look, that's just not going to happen." I said, "It looks like this already, I'll come to set like this."' Over the course of the *Twilight* series, it has been noted by the actor that his hair continues to gain attention to the point of distraction. 'I'm doing fight scenes and there's a strand going down my forehead and they're like, "We need to do it again because no one will recognize you! No one will know who it is!" I have to look like the poster at all times. Just in case they want to use any clip for the trailer. Any clip at all! There were about five people in different departments who, because of my forelock, ended up in tears.'

Because it at times seemed like an entire team was dedicated to monitoring Robert's bronze-tipped locks, the make-up department naturally waited for decisions to be made so they could complement the effort. 'Edward's description in the novel is impossibly handsome, almost god-like,' said *Twilight* make-up artist Jeanne Van Phue. 'His skin is marble-pale, hard as stone and ice cold, but perfect and flawless. Edward's eyes are described as topaz colored when he is normal and black like onyx when hungry.' Van Phue had Robert Pattinson wear colored contact lenses during filming in order to achieve the fluctuation between golden and black eyes described in the novels. Yet the experience quickly became an uncomfortable one for the actor, who later said, 'I have very sensitive eyes, so it took, like, twenty minutes to get in the contacts every single day. People said you get used to it after a while, but after three and a half months, it never, ever got better. It also limits you... it's like you have these masks on your eyes, which take away the life from them, which is very frustrating sometimes. You just have to be shot and look like you're expressionless.'

All of the Cullens and predatory vampires required a pale complexion, but Hardwicke did not want the make-up department to give the characters a macabre appearance, similar to the ones created for Johnny Depp in *Sweeney Todd* or the characters in *Interview with the Vampire*. And while Van Phue chose a dense white coverage for the supporting vampires of *Twilight*, she opted for an altogether subtler approach when it came to Edward Cullen, so as not to disguise Robert Pattinson's natural good looks. 'Edward is the hero, so I had to make him look the best out of everyone,' Van Phue said. 'Rob [already] looks drop-dead gorgeous, so I applied his make-up a little thinner. The pale make-up takes the life out of you, so I let a tiny bit of his natural skin tone come through. I made his eyes more beautiful and put a little lip stain to make him look appealing. Rob looks different from the others; we wanted him to stand out.'

While the make-up and wardrobe departments had their plans in place for the film, Robert Pattinson himself needed to focus on character development and capturing both the physical and emotional foundations of becoming Edward Cullen. He arrived in Oregon two months before the production team and other actors. Cut off from his friends and family, he spent long hours working out in the gym and exploring the depths of Edward Cullen's innermost thoughts. On a physical level, Robert felt the need to push himself to get into shape and give a fair representation of Edward Cullen's perfect body. He spent eight weeks toughening up and developing a chiseled physique, working on a custom exercise program and maintaining a strict, healthy diet. However, he may have taken his athletic ambitions a little too far. When producers arrived three weeks prior to shooting, according to Pattinson, they asked him, 'What are you doing? You look like an alien!' *Entertainment Weekly* later reported that Pattinson's physique had changed so much prior to filming that producers forced him to stop exercising and indulge in cheeseburgers and fatty foods. 'I literally stopped exercising,' Robert recalled. 'Eating a cheeseburger after two and a half months of doing that, it tasted like ambrosia.' During the taping of the DVD commentary for *Twilight*, Robert spoke briefly about this setback, and while commenting on the film's meadow scene, he responds to Edward Cullen's question, 'What do vampires eat?' by shouting out 'cheeseburgers' over Bella's response.

Meanwhile, producers had revisited Robert's headshots and reported back to Hardwicke that they were unsatisfied with the actor's teeth, saying that his smile was not quite perfect enough to represent Stephenie Meyer's literary descriptions. 'They wanted me to have the perfect smile,' Robert said. 'I never thought anything was wrong with my teeth. But the producers still wanted me to wear a brace.' Robert had expensive dental work done prior to filming, appeasing the producers without any complaints. He seemed to recognize it as one more sacrifice that would have to be made in order to portray Catherine Hardwicke's vision of teenage perfection. 'That was the thing in the book, the key thing was that he be attractive,' Robert said. 'And it was especially challenging when you're trying to be frightening and pretty at the same time. It's quite a complicated scenario, especially when you have to stay PG-13.'

His teeth were reset, his hair was ready to be yanked and pulled in numerous directions, and his body was now adjusting to off-and-on workout programs, but certain individuals connected with the production were *still* picking at the most minute flaws in Pattinson's appearance. The criticism, however, came as no surprise to Robert, who explained: 'When you read the book, it seems physically impossible to play the part because Edward is basically just an enigma. He's a canvas for people to project whatever their fantasies about the perfect man are. Being a real human being, you're obviously not going to be everybody's taste.' Although he didn't physically transform into Edward in every way ('I was supposed to get a six-pack,' he confessed. 'But it didn't really work out'), Pattinson still had to spend an immense amount of time developing the tormented persona of Edward Cullen. In order to find Edward's voice, he employed the same technique that had worked so well in his audition, attempting to gain a deeper understanding of the damned nature of eternal life – especially one that had lasted decades without love.

'I did the audition and what people said about why my audition was apparently good was because it was a lot more pained,' Robert said. 'So I built on the fact that he was tortured by various different things.' Robert started by reading the *Twilight* script relentlessly and immersing himself in Meyer's unpublished draft of *Midnight Sun*, although the latter didn't have as much of an impact on his performance as one might expect. '*Midnight Sun* didn't really influence my performance,' Pattinson said. 'I always found that girls are more attracted to the dangerous, the wrong. And so I wanted to put in as much of the dangerous factor of Edward's state into the performance. He's very tightly wound in a lot of places and also there's a fury inside him, and a rage which he has very, very little control over. A lot of which was in *Midnight Sun*. The only thing that I really needed to know was the extent of [his] reaction when he first met Bella, which was in the first chapter. When he was very much considering killing her – he's weighing up the option of killing the entire school just so that he can kill her and there's no witnesses. And he said that, he's not saying it like it's a very distant possibility, he has to make his mind up about the whole situation in a matter of seconds. I kind of want to put that more into the performance.'

But early on it was evident that this role would require more than watching a series of vampire films, lifting weights or staying out of the sun for a few weeks. Robert truly had to search the darkest depths of his psyche to find the same isolation that permeated the pages of Meyer's stories. 'I hadn't realized how difficult it was going to be to play Edward until I started reading the script,' said Pattinson. 'He's a very complex character, so I moved to Portland [Oregon] by myself two or three months before filming began and didn't do anything but read the script and books to find anything that helped me play him. Then I started to write things.' He kept a journal and spent long hours writing dark, emotional letters from Edward to his father asking why Carlisle had ever converted him, condemning him to an eternity of solitude and self-loathing. 'I wanted to feel his isolation,' Robert said. The letters soon became even darker, ranging into Edward's thoughts of suicide – anything that might help him capture the morose torment felt by his on-screen alter ego. 'If you really prepare for a role, there's going to be a moment in which he's all you can think of. So I did things like [write] little suicide notes. I was a little worrisome, actually,' Robert said with a laugh.

Robert also began researching other films and characters in the hope that they'd enrich his own portrayal. Hardwicke had always envisaged Edward as a biker from the wrong side of the tracks, and so Robert looked to a less likely source for inspiration, taking James Dean's classic performance in *Rebel Without a Cause* as the basis of his character. The 1955 film directed by Nicholas Ray tells the story of a rebellious teenager played by James Dean, who relocates to a new town, meets a girl, disobeys his parents and defies the bullies at his high school. '*Rebel Without a Cause* was a big influence on the first [*Twilight* film] – it influenced the hairdo and stuff,' Robert said. 'In lots of ways, it has a very similar character arc: an everyday girl brings this relatively strange individual out of his slump.' Robert would later reveal how he analyzed every last detail of Dean's character, picking up on the mannerisms and trying to incorporate the most minor details into his portrayal of Edward Cullen. 'I just tried to humanize him as much as possible, and then added elements of male personalities, who girls have been attracted to for a long time. I analyzed the lasting appeal of James Dean and tried to incorporate that into the character. I had tons of little things, but that was the kind of vague idea.'

By the time that the rest of the production team and cast had arrived to shoot the film, Robert was excitedly waiting to share his ideas on how to expand the film beyond the horror-teen-romance label. Wishing to shun Edward's idealized qualities as found in the novels, he said, 'I was just thinking how I can abandon this thing about him being the perfect guy, first of all, and about the way he looks and everything. I basically started off saying that okay, "Bella is obsessed and completely infatuated by him, so he could be whatever."'

Upon arrival, producers were greatly impressed by the amount of time Pattinson had spent developing Cullen's brooding personality. 'Robert Pattinson did so much personal work to create a character who has been emotionally dead for a hundred years, but is reawakened by Bella,' said producer Wyck Godfrey. 'He created a whole new life for this character that went above and beyond the call of duty. You had to be sensitive around him, because it was kind of a dark and sad place to be. Catherine and everyone gave Pattinson and Stewart space to do these very intimate scenes. There was the pain and addictive quality of him basically wanting to just reach over and kill Bella, an impulse he's fighting every moment he's with her. Rob played the character as being tortured, which is really the metaphor for young love – it hurts, it's great, it's maddening. He brought that element to it. He becomes obsessed with her, the same way she is with him.'

But not everyone was pleased with Robert taking liberties with the character. It was soon reported that he debated with Stephenie Meyer for many hours over how Edward should be portrayed in the film compared to how he was written in the novel. Robert said, 'I was talking to Stephenie Meyer saying, "The guy must be chronically depressed," and she was saying, "No, he's not, he's not, he's not." But I still maintain that he was. I mean, it's not like depressed, but just this sort of loneliness. I mean, when you see him at school he doesn't really talk to anyone. He must get bored after a while, only hanging out with the same four people in his life.'

Robert Pattinson said that he'd come to dislike Meyer's 'perfect' Edward character during the course of his research. In turn, he reimagined the character as a manic-depressive who hates himself, reflecting the manner in which he'd portrayed Edward during his private audition. Worse still, Robert couldn't shake the impression that he was looking deep into Stephenie Meyer's fantasies while reading the novels. 'I was just convinced that this woman is mad,' said Robert. 'She's completely mad, and she's in love with her own fictional creation.' Given Robert's dark and decidedly morose interpretation of Edward, certain reports suggested that Pattinson and Meyer 'fell out' over the discrepancy.

However, those rumors were soon quelled when Meyer explained that the entire situation was little more than a misunderstanding. 'With Rob, we sat down and talked about Edward's character before the filming started,' Meyer said. 'It wasn't an argument, but we [did] actually disagree on his character. I'd be like, "No, this is how it is." He's like, "No, it's definitely this way." Yet in the performance he did what he wanted, and yet it was exactly what I wanted.'

Still, as filming began it became increasingly evident that Pattinson had gone a bit too far in his character development – at least according to director Catherine Hardwicke and co-star Kristen Stewart. As producer Godfrey said, Robert had reached a dark and sad place – one he was showing no signs of leaving when the cameras stopped rolling. In an attempt to lighten Robert's mood, producers followed him around during downtime, highlighting passages from the book in which Edward actually smiles. 'It was like, "Argh! I was going to smile at some point,"' Robert said. 'Or everyone would be like, "Well, let's try to make this bit funnier!" But it wasn't funny. I tried to play it, as much as possible, like a seventeen-year-old boy who had this purgatory inflicted on him. I just thought, "How would you play this part if it wasn't a teen book adaptation?"'

Kristen Stewart also laughed that Robert had a difficult time going back and forth between the torment of Edward and his own personality while on set. 'I had this little thing,' Stewart said, '"Rob, let's just rehearse the scene all the way through without tearing it down and criticizing it." We'd get two lines out, and then he would say, "No, no, no, it's not working!" Rob made himself crazy the whole movie, and I just stopped and patted him on the back through his neuroses. He would punch me in the face if he heard me right now.'

But Robert felt it necessary to remain in character at all times, stating that Edward needed to be fully aware of danger and his surroundings given Bella's increasing vulnerability. 'When his life is put into basic terms, he has nothing to live for and all he wants to do is either become a human or die,' Robert said. 'The only reason that he hasn't died is because he is too scared; he doesn't think that he has a soul. Then he meets Bella, who makes him feel like a human and feel alive again. At the same time, her human vulnerability makes him incredibly vulnerable, because even with his super speed and his super strength, he still can't fully protect her. Whenever she is in danger, he is in danger. If she dies or goes anywhere, then he is gone, too.'

Though Robert at times acted moodily and sullenly on the set, there were many memorable moments that stood out from the first production, which offered some respite from the serious attitude adopted by the young star. Hardwicke kept the mood light by ribbing Robert about his baseball skills and trying to get him to look like a baseball player, even though the Londoner knew little of the sport and had the lack of skills to match. The baseball game is a critical scene in the movie, particularly known for its special effects and the plot device that ultimately leads to the showdown with James and Victoria. During the vampire game itself, Edward Cullen is supposed to appear perfectly comfortable on the baseball diamond, given his decades of playing games in lightning storms with his family. However, that comfort on the field was completely foreign to Robert Pattinson. 'I'm terrible [at baseball],' said Robert. 'I'm completely mal-coordinated. I'm terrible at all sports. Also, I don't see the point as well.'

It was clear that Robert felt worse than a fish out of water in the baseball scenes. So determined was Hardwicke to make Edward Cullen the star player in the game that she brought in a coach to help train Pattinson. Shortly after he began doing publicity events for *Twilight*, interviews consistently included a question or two about his discomfort on the field. 'I've been asked this everywhere. "So I understand you're crap at baseball . . ." I just didn't care,' Robert said. 'I think sports are stupid. Catherine Hardwicke was so determined to make me look like a professional baseball player. She had this coach trying to teach me the "ready" position, like a little squat. I was like, "Seriously, I'll do it on the day. You don't have to teach me." But Catherine wanted to see it, in front of all these extras. It was just very embarrassing. So for the rest of the shoot, whenever Catherine couldn't decide how to block a shot I'd say, "I think I should be doing my ready position." But yeah, I'm terrible at baseball. I'm terrible at every sport apart from running, but I'm terrible at that now too.'

While Hardwicke's enforced baseball practice may have been an attempt to raise morale on set – getting Rob to take his role a little less seriously – it was equally a test of the young actor's ability to keep up with direction and criticism in order to complete the task at hand. Also, despite the tension caused by Robert's liberal portrayal of the romantic literary figure, Hardwicke was willing to allow him a certain license to ad-lib, choosing dialogue to suit particular scenes in the film. One of *Twilight*'s most iconic lines is delivered as Bella wraps both arms around Edward's back before the couple shoot up into the trees. 'You'd better hold on tight, spider monkey,' quickly became a sensation among fans, inspiring a plethora of websites, T-shirts and fan tributes. Hardwicke admits that it was Pattinson who chose this line from eight different options prior to shooting.

While *Twilight* was in production, Hollywood came to a standstill because of a massive writers' strike, barring screenwriter Melissa Rosenberg from offering any input into the script so long as union leaders were still renegotiating interactive royalties with studios. Knowing she couldn't wait for Rosenberg's dialogue concepts for this romantic scene, Hardwicke herself scribbled approximately ten ideas into the margin of the shooting script before handing the list to Pattinson. 'I gave it to Rob, the whole list,' said Hardwicke. 'And I said, "Rob, which one do you want to say?" And he goes, "I want to say the spider-monkey one."'

The line itself was far better and more original than the alternatives, which included, 'You're not scared of heights, are you?' 'Got a good grip? Don't let go,' and, 'Prepare for liftoff.' Months after the film's release, Hardwicke championed Robert's decision, saying, 'It's a fun line. Thank god he picked that one.'

Though Robert was deeply entrenched in the mind of his character, it was the opportunity to offer creative input of this variety that instilled in him a deep appreciation of working with Hardwicke. Given her blunt attention to detail and willingness to do repeat takes, Hardwicke created a professional environment unlike any Robert had known before. 'She's such a free spirit,' Robert said of the *Twilight* director. 'She has no filter. She kind of gets you out of nowhere. Like she'd go, "You know that thing you're doing there? Yeah, that. That's not good." And I'd go, "Really?" And she'd say, "Yeah. It's weird. And it's not working. At all." The diplomacy department is not her finest. But you love that about her, that she feels free to say, "That sucked. Try something else." She wouldn't say I "sucked" but she'd go, "That's too big, too over the top. Try something subtler," which is really her way of saying that you sucked.'

As filming progressed and Robert continued to devour the script, he would occasionally be struck by facets of Edward's character that he'd never quite realized before – even during his time alone in Oregon. 'What I never really understood about his attractiveness, especially to young girls, is his gentlemanliness,' he mused. 'I thought that teenage girls like the dangerous aspect of males, and so I tried to emphasize the danger and make the more gentlemanly side of this character a veil to something else underneath. I really tried to make him an incredibly strong and powerful character, but at the same time self-loathing and extremely vulnerable.'

With the guidance of Catherine Hardwicke and her team, along with several months of preparation, Robert Pattinson created the perfect on-screen Edward Cullen, a distinctly charming-yet-dark character whose remarkable good looks and protective instincts would capture the hearts of every member of the continually expanding Team Edward. But with three *Twilight Saga* films now complete, and reported plans to split *Breaking Dawn* into two additional productions, fans might question how directors and producers aim to maintain Edward's timeless seventeen-year-old existence in the final segments. What tricks could producers and make-up artists possibly have up their sleeves in order to keep the character looking forever young?

'Botox,' laughed Robert. 'No, actually I am a bit worried about that. I don't know, I guess we'll have to shoot them pretty quickly.'

10

Pattinson on tour

'I've been going for the last three weeks, just going to different cities all
around the world, just to get to these planned mobbings, where everybody just
screams and screams and screams.'
– Robert Pattinson

Prior to his *Twilight* audition, low-key Londoner Robert Pattinson was hardly 100 percent committed to the idea of filming another big-budget blockbuster – particularly after his experience on *Harry Potter and the Goblet of Fire*. He was too attached to his relaxed lifestyle, playing open-mic nights around Soho with the 'Brit Pack' while he continued to hone his acting skills. 'At first I didn't want to do a movie like *Twilight*,' he said. 'I specifically hadn't done anything that anyone would see since *Harry Potter* because I wanted to teach myself how to act. I didn't want to be an idiot.'

Fortunately for the millions of *Twilight* fans who would soon become devoted to him, Robert changed his mind after his first reading with Kristen Stewart, his confidence in the project boosted by the instant chemistry he shared with his future co-star. It is now difficult to imagine any other actor embodying Edward Cullen, and one can only wonder how the film would have been received without Robert, or where Pattinson would be now had he turned down the role or been rejected by Catherine Hardwicke. 'I was going to wait for another year to do two or three more little things and then do something bigger,' he said. '*Twilight* came kind of randomly. It was a chance, and as I didn't have a reputation at all there was nothing for me to lose.'

Of course, during the film's pre-production, no one involved with *Twilight* could have predicted that they were making the first part of what would become one of the most successful movie franchises in recent history, nor the stratospheric level of fame it would bestow upon its lead actors. 'I don't even think the people who own the rights to the books knew this would happen, and it keeps getting bigger,' Robert said. 'The book sales have gone up since the movies came out. And the fan stories get more and more passionate.'

Since the moment Stephenie Meyer endorsed Robert for the role of

Edward, he has been at the center of a media storm that has not stopped raging – and nor will it cease to any time in the near future. In just two years, Robert Pattinson has progressed from a respected – but hardly recognized – indie actor to a global superstar who induces a decibel increase whenever he enters a room. At times, though, Robert does seem overwhelmed by the phenomenon, vainly attempting to emphasize that he is just a small part of a global franchise that producers and actors alike grossly underestimated from the beginning.

Early on, after the release of *Twilight*, it was clear that sudden fame had startled Robert to some degree. The whirlwind promotional tour required laps around the world, hundreds of interviews per week, and countless TV appearances – all part of an endless schedule that would tire any person obliged to engage in it. Even after several months of personal appearances, he still didn't understand the feverish intensity of fan interest surrounding the fictitious vampire Edward Cullen or, more importantly, Robert Pattinson. At the San Diego Comic-Con convention in July 2008 he had his first experience of fans' devotion to his character, but was scarcely prepared for their reaction to himself. 'Until the moment I walked on stage, I had no idea,' he said, 'then they put the word "*Twilight*" on the screen, and 7,000 girls were screaming for forty-five minutes.'

From that moment on, the screaming girls didn't stop showing up to any event he attended, be it a *Twilight* promotional appearance or even his exiting a restaurant after a quiet dinner. For Robert, the promotional events were 'fascinating'. 'You'd have two or three minutes to affect someone. Make them hear you. Get the message out and maybe it will echo,' he said. 'I quite enjoyed doing press for the first *Twilight*, because there was a similarity [to political communications, which he had considered as a career path before becoming an actor]. But after a bit I was ladling it out. If you want people to listen to you, you'd better have something to say. I felt a responsibility to be fascinating. You're bargaining with the audience. Is this enough for them? And that affects the way you look at art.'

Nevertheless, the mob-like crowding that became an inevitable part of promotional events began to wear on him relatively quickly. Several events throughout the United States had to be canceled because of the potentially dangerous numbers of fans with whom security were ill-equipped to deal. In November 2008, a 'meet and greet' and autograph session in San Francisco was canceled when a crowd of roughly 3,000 fans turned violent, overwhelming the lone security guard who'd been hired for the event. One girl was bloodied and numerous others injured when they were shoved during the ensuing chaos. The same level of hysteria unfolded that year at the NYC Apple Store where Robert was supposed to be signing autographs. This event was also canceled.

'I don't know why it still shocks me,' he said of his close encounters with hysterical fans. 'I mean, I've been going for the last three weeks, just going to different cities all around the world, just to get to these planned mobbings, where everybody just screams and screams and screams. But every single time, I get so nervous, and kind of cold sweats, and everything. So I doubt that I am ready.'

As Robert's fame began to rise, other members of the cast noticed the stress weighing on the young actor. 'Every second of Rob's life is watched now,' Kellan Lutz said, explaining that Robert changes his schedule on a regular basis in order to try to avoid the increased scrutiny of fans and paparazzi. 'I'm sure he's careful for everything he's doing.'

Peter Facinelli, who plays Robert's on-screen father Carlisle Cullen, revealed that even Robert's most basic errands were commonly interrupted by *Twilight* fever. 'I've talked to Rob about it, and he's just paranoid all the time now,' Facinelli said. 'Like, even to go down to the Starbucks, he's ducking behind cars and does a roll-flip to the coffee shop. Then he gets up, and there's nobody there – but then the one time that he doesn't do that, that's when there's like 10,000 paparazzi jumping out of the bushes.'

By mid-2009, reports began to circulate that Pattinson was so overwhelmed by the constant attention that he couldn't wait to get back to London, where he felt that he could detach himself from the franchise. 'Robert is dying to get back home,' a friend confessed. 'He's so over everything. He's overwhelmed by all the girls. They terrify him. He says girls grab his neck and clothing all of the time, and he's not used to that. Fans don't do that to him in London. Everyone there is a little cooler about the fame thing, which is what he's used to.'

But the screaming fans weren't confined to the United States, and Robert continued to feel the pressure as he moved from country to country. While traveling around Italy to promote *Twilight*, the actor broke down, feeling he'd completely lost control. 'I started crying in Italy,' he said. 'Like, completely involuntarily. It was really embarrassing. I didn't even know I was. Kristen, I think, turned around to me. And she's like, "Are you crying?" When you're in a situation that feels like it's gotten out of control, I find that the more you stress out about it, the worse it would get.' The public frenzy surrounding Robert Pattinson wasn't something he had anticipated, and it has grown exponentially with each subsequent release of the *Twilight* series. Preparations for *Eclipse*'s arrival in cinemas will involve the same intense level of security that trails the cast everywhere, as Team-Edward fever begins to ignite.

Robert's attempts to distance himself from his fans may be the result of a string of somewhat bizarre encounters. Pattinson told E! Online that a seven-year-old girl had asked him to bite her. 'It wasn't a joke,' he said. 'I looked at her and thought, "Do you know what you're saying?"' Robert, of course, turned down the request, but the story was frequently recounted in the press during the course of the film's promotion.

During the filming of *Twilight*, a fan handed their infant to an assistant and asked that the child be photographed with the cast while the parent stood behind the barriers of the set. 'A while back, somebody gave me a baby to keep, and I kept it and renamed him,' Robert said with a laugh on *The Ellen DeGeneres Show* in 2009. 'It was on the set of the first film, and they just freely handed a baby to a PA and they brought it round to have photos taken with the cast.'

Another incident saw a female Pattinson fan attempt to take off all of her clothes in a roomful of people after the actor joked that it was an easy way to get his attention. 'It was after a period of signing 500 signatures and one of them came up and you only have ten seconds with each person and you never really say anything. And I kind of got a bit bored of just saying, "Hey, hey. How are you doing?" And she said in her ten seconds, what can I do to get your attention, and I was just like, "Just take your clothes off." And [she] stood there and frantically started taking her clothes off and got dragged out of the room by security. I've never felt more terrible.'

For Robert one of the most difficult parts of being a star is finding a way to properly respond to each unusual request. There was another incident involving a small child and a fan who didn't appear to comprehend the difference between Robert Pattinson and Edward Cullen: 'A mother recently gave me her baby and asked, "Can you please bite his head?"'

Robert has occasionally spoken about unusual pieces of fan mail that he receives: 'Letters that say, "I'm going to kill myself if you don't watch *High School Musical 2* with me."' In addition, the actor once found a series of unnerving notes on his car, left there for him by female fans. 'There was a group of girls that left little notes in my car, outside of my apartment,' he said. 'One of the first notes said: "I'm not weird, but please call me." The next day the note said: "Please don't ignore me." And the next day it said: "I'm going to kill myself if you keep ignoring me! (But I'm not weird, okay?)."'

As the requests have become more unusual over time, Robert has grown concerned about his safety given the near-constant presence of people who follow him from place to place and stand outside his home and hotels. 'My brain doesn't really accept fame,' he said, 'so it's fine. I can be put anywhere and it just goes completely over my head. I just don't want to get shot or stabbed. I don't want someone to have a needle and I'll get AIDS afterwards. That's my only real fear. Whenever I see a crowd I always think that. It's like being on a plane. I think the bottom is going to hit the runway when it's taking off.'

But despite the list of unusual requests, as he has progressed through shooting the series Robert Pattinson has, over time, begun to see a lighter side of *Twilight* mania. His concerns about his safety aside, he believes that fans are not 'crazy', but rather just devoted supporters of *The Twilight Saga* novels and films. The fans who come to the sets to express their appreciation and meet him and the rest of the cast remind Robert of exactly why he's able to be part of such a dynamic and successful franchise. 'Everybody's always saying, "Oh, those obsessive fans." I remember a few weeks ago, I was shooting *Eclipse* and there were just two women standing outside the set and they were standing there for two or three days, all day. And I always drove past thinking, like, "Oh those guys must be weirdoes." And on the last day we were at that location. I think Jackson Rathbone got out and said hello to them. And it was right in front of me and they knew that I was in the car behind. I got out and started talking to them. It's so strange when you think you get cut off from everyone and you suddenly realize these people are only here because they love the books and the films, and that's all there is to it. There's nothing weird to it,' Robert said. He explained that because he was working so intensely, shooting for twelve to fourteen hours a day, he hadn't realized quite how appreciative fans were of an autograph and the opportunity to briefly chat with him. 'People just wait there. Nothing could please them more than just two minutes talking to you.'

Because of *Twilight* Robert has experienced both intense fan support and somewhat obsessive and bizarre behavior. 'There are good and bad sides of everything. Of course I don't regret it, but everything isn't perfect either. If no one knows who you are, it is difficult to land a role and it sucks because you feel like a loser. When you become someone, everyone expects a miracle from you, big roles, big movies, big hits, and it is not easy because it is a big responsibility, big pressure. It's always the best to be in the middle.'

But for now, while the young actor recognizes that many fans see him solely as Edward Cullen, he hopes that over time he will be able to distance himself from the franchise and establish a career as one of Hollywood's elite actors. 'You just have to wait and see how people will take you. If people still see me as Edward Cullen in twenty-five years, I think I might have to murder someone.' Self-deprecating as ever, Robert Pattinson does fear that *Twilight* fans might desert him after the final film is released, potentially in 2011. 'If it suddenly dies down and suddenly no one is interested . . . yeah, it is worrying,' he said. 'It's scary to think that it all might just fundamentally stop after the *Twilight* thing's finished.' It's a challenge that any actor in a major franchise faces, and Robert's concern that people will forever identify him with Edward Cullen is warranted. Still, even if his fame were to diminish, he remains certain of one thing about his future. 'My attitude from the beginning has been, "If you start failing, do not start going on reality TV shows."'

11

Life Without Edward

'He's the hero of the story that just refuses to accept that
he's the hero, and I think that's kind of admirable.'
– Robert Pattinson

Summit Entertainment's $37-million investment in the first *Twilight* film clearly paid off, garnering a gross return of more than ten times the original production budget. It was an immense success from a financial and critical standpoint – to say the very least – as Twi-hards around the world devoured Catherine Hardwicke's adaptation and showered it with rave reviews. One week prior to *Twilight*'s premiere in November 2008, Summit formally revealed that it had optioned the film rights to Stephenie Meyer's three subsequent novels, *New Moon*, *Eclipse* and *Breaking Dawn*. Two days after *Twilight* hit theaters across the United States, the production company announced that it would soon be reuniting the cast for the second installment of the franchise, *New Moon*, which was scheduled for release in mid-November 2009.

The firmly established relationship between the author and the production team fueled a strong enthusiasm for the sequels, as Meyer herself raved about her experience working on the first film. 'I don't think any other author has had a more positive experience with the makers of her movie adaptation than I have had with Summit Entertainment,' said Meyer in the written announcement of *New Moon*'s future release. 'I'm thrilled to have the chance to work with them again on *New Moon*.' While Taylor Lautner faced the challenge of putting on thirty pounds of muscle to retain the role of Jacob Black, the major change to production for the sequel was that Catherine Hardwicke would be replaced as director. In mid-December 2008, Summit announced that Academy-Award-nominated writer, director and producer Chris Weitz would be helming the shoot of Melissa Rosenberg's script.

New Moon begins with Bella Swan turning eighteen. Reluctantly, she agrees to attend a party thrown by the Cullens in her honor. For Bella, this birthday is a painful reminder of how her vampire beau will stay young forever while her own youth continues to slip away, while to Edward's mind the event marks another incredible milestone in the couple's budding romance. Her would-be in-laws shower her with presents, welcoming her as one of their own in a moment that Bella has wished for since meeting them a year earlier. 'The birthday scene at the Cullen house is like the ideal birthday party,' said Rob Pattinson. 'The house is beautifully decorated and everyone is very happy. Edward is looking at Bella and thinking that she can become part of his family and his life – that maybe this can work out the way he it wants to.'

But the party ends quickly as – in a tragic twist – Bella gets a paper cut when opening one of the perfectly wrapped gifts, and a single drop of her blood falls on the carpet. Unable to contain his blood lust, Edward's adopted brother Jasper rushes to attack Bella. Edward fights him off, but, in the process, the two vampires destroy the living room, and Bella is left with a gushing wound on her arm after cutting it on broken glass. The rest of the Cullens, with the exception of Carlisle and Edward, rush out of the room to avoid the tempting scent of Bella's blood.

As Carlisle tends to Bella's arm, she points out that these ongoing mishaps would not happen if Edward changed her into a vampire and fully welcomed her into the Cullen family. But Carlisle reveals the true reason that Edward refuses to give her eternal life: Edward believes that vampires are soulless beings who cannot pass on to the afterlife and are damned for eternity. Edward does not wish this torture upon his true love.

Jasper's near-fatal attack shows the fragility of the trust between the human Bella and the vampire family. While Bella dismisses the event as a squabble among the Cullens (similar to Rosalie's outbursts in the first novel), Edward remains shaken by the event, his fear for his girlfriend's safety intensifying. Promising her that it will be as if he never existed, Edward makes up his mind to disappear from her life in order to ensure her protection. It is a moment that shatters Bella's heart and her dreams of eternal life and love. The break-up scene is Pattinson's most critical moment in the film, as it sets the tone for the rest of the story and leads to his later sporadic appearances in Bella's visions. Robert Pattinson would later suggest that this scene is so heart-wrenching because it's a moment that *Twilight* fans – those who view Edward and Bella's love as the perfect literary and film romance – would react to it with a pain similar to that felt by the heroine when the vampire leaves her. 'There's something weird about [the break-up of Bella and Edward],' Robert said. 'One of the main things I felt doing that, and what really helped, was people's anticipation of the movie, and the fans of the series' idea about what Bella and Edward's relationship is and what it represents to them. It's some kind of ideal for a relationship. And so, just playing a scene where you're breaking up the ideal relationship, I felt a lot of the weight behind that. Also, it took away a fear of melodrama. It felt seismic, even when we were doing it. It was very much like the stepping out into the sunlight scene, at the end. You could really feel the audience watching, as you're doing it. It was a strange one to do.'

Of course, filming the scene would not be an easy task simply because of the emotional demands it placed upon Robert Pattinson and Kristen Stewart. During the shoot, the actor was constantly pestered by a different species of bloodsucker eager to get a taste of Robert Pattinson. 'I was filming the break-up scene with Bella, this big, traumatic scene, and there was like, literally, a plague of mosquitoes,' said Robert. 'I'd never seen so many mosquitoes in my entire life, and giant ones, as well. I could just tell when a mosquito was on the end of my nose and not be able to do anything about it. And they did not stop landing on us all night. So it was not my favorite scene to film, but it was funny.'

After Edward and his family disappear from Forks, Bella's life and heart are shattered. She dissolves into a dark, zombie-like depression for several months, wondering if the pain in her chest and mind will ever heal. But one day, she feels a small amount of joy after discovering that she can hear Edward's voice in her head while she's engaging in reckless behavior, as he warns her against risk-taking and advises her on how to escape from dangerous situations. Bella, of course, elects to continue to engage in such irresponsible activities, just to hear the sound of Edward's voice again. But with Edward out of the picture, and Bella now seeking a motorcycle mechanic, she begins an innocent relationship with the vampire's rival, the Quileute Jacob Black. Jacob sees Edward's disappearance as an exclusive opportunity to steal Bella's heart from his cold-blooded competition. As Bella and Jacob begin a series of adventures, Edward remains a torturous siren in her head, reminding her of the dissolution of a romance she believed would last for eternity.

Robert Pattinson jumped at the opportunity to reprise the role of Edward, even though he laughed on several occasions that 'Edward is hardly in it'. Despite his lack of screen time in the sequel, Robert was savvy enough to realize his long-term importance to the franchise, fully aware that Summit had made significant investments in the third and fourth novels in the series. As Pattinson began to look at his role in the second film, the actor reflected on *New Moon*'s importance in shaping his original interpretation of the character. Shortly after the film's production was announced in 2008, Rob immersed himself in the second novel.

He began to recognize the dramatic change in Edward's portrayal in the sequel and sought to bring this natural evolution alive on-screen. 'When I read *New Moon*, it gave me ideas about how to play him in the first film. It's the one I connected to the most, and the one that humanized Edward for me the most, as well. In the first one, he still does remain, from beginning to end, an idealistic character. But, in the second one, he makes a mistake that's acknowledged by everybody, including himself. Also, he is totally undermined by more powerful creatures, and he's undermined emotionally by people as well. That's what humanized it. Since I read that book, I always liked him as a character, and I've tried to play that same feeling throughout the films. He's the hero of the story that just refuses to accept that he's the hero, and I think that's kind of admirable.'

The more Robert read the novel, the more he began to see traits of his own personality in Edward. When asked by Cole Haddon of Film.com about which characteristics he shares with Cullen, one immediately sprang to mind. 'I guess stubbornness, in some ways, about some things. [Edward]'s pretty self-righteous. I get quite obsessive about things and possessive as well,' Robert said. 'I have very, very specific ideas about how I want to do my work and how I want to be perceived, to the point of ridiculousness sometimes. I don't listen to anyone else. That's why I don't have a publicist or anything. I can't stand it if someone is trying to tell me to do something, which is maybe a mistake sometimes. I like being meticulous, and it's quite difficult, as an actor, to have that much control. The good thing about the *Twilight* series is that it does give you a lot more control over little things, which I want to have. I'm a control freak about it.'

In the novel *New Moon*, Bella's repeated reckless and dangerous behavior coaxes Edward's voice into her mind, as he warns her to stop, or advises how she should react to potential threats. Of course, most of the time, Bella is only living on the edge to hear her love's voice. A major question for new director Chris Weitz and the production team was how they would could incorporate Edward's mental warnings to Bella into the film. 'It is interesting,' said screenwriter Melissa Rosenberg. 'He [Edward] isn't physically in *New Moon* a lot, but he is very much a presence throughout the book. That was the challenge of the script, how to keep him alive in the same way the book does and stay true to the book. I think we found a way to do that.'

The production team decided to make Edward an on-screen vision when Bella hears his warnings, rather than just a series of voiceovers. Robert was naturally concerned about how this would be conducted, as the producers had been extremely committed to creating a faithful adaptation of the original novel. 'I was always very worried about that. Even before we started shooting, people were asking questions and saying, "Oh, are you worried that people will think there's not enough Edward in it?" But he's not in the book. I was [more] worried that it was just going to be random scenes. There was talk, at the beginning, of showing his backstory in South America, going around moping [after his break-up with Bella]. That would have been terrifying for me, and I think it would have been catastrophic for the film as well. I fought as far as I could to keep it as limited as possible, mainly because it just doesn't happen in the book. But then, at the same time, it's scary just to do a voiceover, because it could end up being very cheesy.'

In order to keep Edward's appearances in the film as faithful to the novel as possible, Pattinson lobbied directly to Weitz. The director promised not to add extra scenes to the film just to increase his screen time and appease Pattinson's fans. 'Even since it's been edited, there were loads and loads of the apparition sequences cut out,' Robert said. 'A lot of them Chris cut out without me saying. But, when I was doing ADR, I was saying, "It will be more interesting and mystical if you cut out more of these shots. It becomes more eerie and more realistic, the less of these visions you have." Just having head-on shots makes it something other than a vision. It becomes a superimposed image, which is not interesting.'

While fans of the film raved about Jacob Black's CGI transformation into a werewolf, it took a comparable degree of special-effects work in order to make Edward's ghostly appearances convincing. To present Edward as an apparition responding to Bella's endangerment, Robert was required to work closely with Chris Weitz and the special-effects team on a green screen, with Edward's sequences later spliced into the film whenever Bella hears his voice. For example, Bella imagines that Edward is following her when she rides on her motorcycle. While shooting that scene, the motorcycle Kristen Stewart rode was attached to a moving trailer that was pulled by a rig. Weitz directed Stewart to turn her head during the shot, and in the finished scene Bella gasps as she catches sight of her lost love while her hair lashes about her face. In order to place Robert in the shot, Weitz and his crew filmed Pattinson on green screen and imposed him as a hazy, flame-like image behind her. As Pattinson explained, the special-effects team 'designed a thing that basically allowed me to stand on a green box and stay relatively expressionless and all these machines did the acting for me. Just the way I like it.'

Since Edward Cullen is mostly absent from the film and novel, the story focuses heavily upon the physical and emotional transformation of Jacob

Black, portrayed by Taylor Lautner, and his relationship with Bella. Lautner, to his credit, fought hard to retain his role as Pattinson's romantic rival in the second film; he underwent a significant transformation of his own, building nearly thirty pounds of muscle to portray the rapidly maturing Quileute teen. Lautner's success immediately generated a buzz around the set, and though it might have made Robert a bit self-conscious, Pattinson wasn't exactly a flabby performer either. 'I didn't see Taylor until just a little bit before we started shooting,' said Robert, 'so when he came back, I had the same reaction as everybody else. I was like, "Now I have to go to the gym."'

During his preparation for the first film, Robert had worked out by himself and overdone the exercise to such an extent that the director, Catherine Hardwicke, forced him to stop lifting weights and start eating cheeseburgers. For *New Moon*, however, Robert worked with Nathan Mellalieu, a Canadian personal trainer who had previously coached Harrison Ford, Halle Berry and Ben Affleck for film roles. Mellalieu's goal was to get the entire cast of vampires and werewolves into quick shape prior to filming. 'When they came to Vancouver – where *New Moon* was filmed – some of the actors were fitter than others. Kellan Lutz, who plays one of the most ripped vampires in the film, was already in good shape, but a few needed more attention. Everyone had a tailored routine that would keep them motivated and develop the parts of their body that needed work,' said Mellalieu. 'We wanted the vampires to look like supermodels and the werewolves to look brawny and rugged.'

Robert quickly toned up, shedding excess bulk and developing the foundation of his own abdominal six-pack to rival Lautner's shredded physique. 'With Robert Pattinson we did lots of boxing drills, which helped create the lean, muscled look he has in *New Moon*. He has great hand speed and footwork and seemed to really enjoy the sessions. We also had all the actors doing functional exercises using little or no weight so they weren't bogged down with too much bulk and could move athletically when filming a stunt.'

As Robert would not be playing the lead in this film, he basked in the comparative lack of pressure he faced upon his arrival in Vancouver. Aside from the confidence afforded by the massive success of the first film, Robert found that he was far more secure about his acting ability in the run up to *New Moon*. 'I was really beating myself up about stuff on the last one, but because of its success, I feel like I kind of know that a couple of things I did were okay. I have some kind of foundation, which I know will at least please an audience . . . maybe.'

Robert attributed part of this reduced sense of pressure to the more laidback on-set environment created by director Chris Weitz. During the months on the shoot, Robert and his co-stars regularly involved themselves in Vancouver's lively bar scene and spent late nights playing instruments and jamming with local musicians. Although the global media regularly followed the cast around the city and stoked rumors of an off-screen relationship between Pattinson and Kristen Stewart, Robert said that he and his cast mates didn't feel that they were under any great pressure or scrutiny from fans and the press while on location. 'It is strange,' Robert said during production of *New Moon*. 'I was having dinner the other day and there was some magazine cover we [he and Kristen] saw. The movie is so insulated; someone was saying it's like being in the eye of the storm, but when you're in it, you can't really see what's going on. It seems like complete calmness. Then you look at magazine covers, and you realize it's actually a real magazine cover with us on and rumors that we're together. It sounds stupid, but people seem to believe it.'

Of course, *New Moon* was more of a showcase for Taylor Lautner. The emergence of warm-blooded lupine Jacob Black as Edward's romantic rival led a number of fans to defect from Team Edward to Team Jacob. However, the story ends with Bella going back to her true love Edward, shortly after she and Alice save him from the Volturi vampires as the film nears its conclusion.

Bella soon realizes that she has developed feelings for Jacob, setting the stage for the love triangle that dominates the storyline of *Eclipse*. Though Pattinson again performed exceptionally in the more limited portrayal of Edward Cullen required for the second film, the actor tried to deflect praise for his performance once again, with claims that *New Moon* had 'nothing to do with [him]'. During an interview with Moviefone, Robert laughed, '[The movie] is not my responsibility. I mean I'm the fourth, fifth, maybe sixth lead. Even the CGI wolf comes before me!'

But director Chris Weitz, who was also partaking in the interview, argued that Rob Pattinson was trying his best to distance himself from the hype and hysteria, knowing full well that *Eclipse* would generate heated debates about Edward Cullen and Jacob Black, or more importantly Robert Pattinson and Taylor Lautner. For more than a year, Robert had been one of the most talked-about young actors in Hollywood. Nonetheless he'd continually shunned the media spotlight, focusing on the collective efforts of everyone involved in the franchise. 'I love that Rob tries to claim he is not in the movie because he basically wants his private life back,' Weitz laughed, turning to Pattinson with a smile. 'It's not going to work, Rob.'

12
the Case for team Edward

'I mean, every vampire story is always about people essentially
wanting to be bitten by vampires. They're kind of seduced into their own death,
which kind of makes it a bit more attractive.'
– Robert Pattinson

In October 2009, director David Slade revealed – to the excitement of
Twi-hards everywhere – that production of *Eclipse*, the third installment
of *The Twilight Saga*, had wrapped in Vancouver. Best known for his edgy
and violent films *Hard Candy* and *30 Days of Night*, Slade might not
have been the obvious choice to replace *New Moon* director Chris Weitz,
particularly in a franchise with such a young target audience. However,
given the darker tone of the novel, which centers on a war between
rival camps of vampires and werewolves, Slade appeared to be a logical
candidate, particularly given Summit Entertainment's desire to make
this latest installment of the series more 'guy-friendly'. In a press release
formally announcing Slade's appointment, Summit's president, Erik Feig,
said, 'Stephenie Meyer's *Eclipse* is a muscular, rich, vivid book, and we
at Summit looked long and hard for a director who could do it justice.
We believe we have found that talent in David Slade, a director who has
been able to create complex, visually arresting worlds. We cannot wait to
see the *Eclipse* he brings to life and brings to the fans eagerly awaiting its
arrival in summer of 2010.'

The film (like the novel) begins not long after Bella and Alice have
rescued Edward from the Volturi, and Edward's promise to turn his love
into a vampire for her own protection – provided that they're married
first. Otherwise, Carlisle offers to do the job as soon as Bella has graduated
from high school. With graduation day fast approaching, Bella begins
making plans to leave Forks under the guise of attending college, when
her true intention is to leave her home and her humanity behind forever.
The moment she has joined Edward and the Cullen coven, she will never
be allowed to return home to her father Charlie. But before any of these
dreams can be realized, Victoria – still seeking to avenge the death of her
murdered mate James – returns to Forks along with her own personal
army of newborns, to threaten the lives of Bella, the Cullens and Jacob,

who has persuaded the wolf pack to fight alongside the Cullen coven in order to prove his worth to Bella. '*Eclipse* isn't as intimate as *Twilight* or *New Moon*,' Robert Pattinson said. 'We're at war, so I get to interact with more characters, not just Kristen. You'll also find out more about the other members of the Cullen family. It just feels bigger.'

While Victoria's thirst for vengeance and the tribal war she engineers as a result are integral elements of the story, the main thrust of both the novel and the film is the heartbreaking love triangle played out between Bella, Edward and Jacob. The bitter rivalry between vampire and werewolf ultimately leaves one of Bella's suitors abandoned.

At the end of *Eclipse*, Bella must make that decision, choosing between her soul mate Edward and her best friend Jacob, both of whom she loves deeply, but each in a unique way. Bella chooses Edward, whom she has loved since the day they met. But to address the much larger debate between rival camps, one must ask if Bella truly makes the right decision? Since *Eclipse* first appeared in print, the theoretical debate over whether Bella should choose the cold-blooded romantic or the furry lupine hunk has unleashed an international battle between two camps of *Twilight* fans, who identify themselves as members of either Team Edward or Team Jacob. 'Bella's choice' is a decision that has been disputed around the world. Everywhere from online message boards to television roundtables, members of Team Edward and Team Jacob have come up against each other in full force whenever this contentious question is so much as mentioned in passing.

Team Edward fans naturally argue that Bella chose correctly in devoting herself to Edward at the end of Meyer's third novel, while Team Jacob fans prefer a revisionist account that would have ended with the heroine in the Quileute's muscular arms. 'I think what's fantastic about Stephenie Meyer's series is she took these mythical creatures, vampires and werewolves, which everyone thinks they know about, and reinvented them,' said Erik Feig. 'And Bella Swan is every girl, but relatable to women and men and all ages. The tug between Edward and Jacob is such a relatable experience.'

The argument for members of Team Edward focuses on Cullen's sterling qualities and the drawbacks of the warm-blooded wolf boy, who often spends too much time with the pack and not enough tending to Bella's needs. Readers who identify themselves as loyal supporters of the cuddly yet fiery lupine might want to avoid the following paragraphs, as they examine Team Edward's belief that Bella made the correct decision in choosing her vampire, and why her selection of Jacob Black would have been an egregious mistake.

Edward Cullen's positive qualities are manifold, but among his most compelling are his remarkable combination of extraordinary good looks and sexy demeanor; his old-fashioned charm, honed by a century on earth; and his preternatural instinct to protect the woman he has loved since he first caught sight of her. According to Bella, Edward Cullen is impossibly beautiful, with perfect teeth and striking features that make it near impossible for any woman to look away when he enters a room. In addition, his being a vampire creates a haunting longing for forbidden pleasure in Bella, his supernaturally seductive qualities making him all the more desirable. 'They've always been a lot to do with sexuality, and temptation, and there's something forbidden about it,' said Robert Pattinson. 'I mean, every vampire story is always about people essentially wanting to be bitten by vampires. They're kind of seduced into their own death, which kind of makes it a bit more attractive.'

Edward is not only described as the most physically beautiful being in the world, but he is also far more cultured than Jacob Black. During his 107 years on earth, he has made the most of his free time. During almost a century of sleepless nights, he has read countless books, completed medical school twice, studied a number of foreign languages, and become a virtuoso pianist. His expansive music collection ranges from jazz to progressive metal to classical. 'Edward's niche [. . .] is music. He knows a lot about music, and has watched how music has changed over the years,' said *Twilight* art director Ian Phillips. *Twilight* depicts the careful attention that Edward pays to his music collection, as it is the only prominent feature of his bedroom; one that he intimately shares with Bella the first time she visits his house.

Edward's attraction to Bella is also far stronger than Jacob's. His description of her as being like an addictive opiate makes clear the enormous physical and psychological torture that he continually undergoes whenever she is near. But for nearly a century, Edward has been longing for the love of a woman like Bella, which makes him capable of resisting his urges. When *The Twilight Saga* begins, he is a tortured soul, filled with self-loathing and plagued by thoughts of death and his own destruction. These feelings fade only as his relationship with Bella blossoms. His restraint around her is evidence of remarkable willpower; his bloodlust is replaced by protective love and an ardent desire for redemption in their future together. 'Edward is kind of a reluctant vampire,' explains Pattinson. 'He's a seventeen-year-old boy who turned into a vampire over a hundred years ago, and he's kind of lost his way in the world. He has no idea what he is, or the point of his existence. Bella Swan opens him up to the world again.'

One of the most compelling arguments deployed by Team Edward is simply that, being a vampire, Edward is capable of transforming, loving and protecting Bella for eternity. Certainly, it is clear what's in his mind as he asks for her hand in marriage, promising to love her 'forever'. Edward can provide eternal life and love for Bella by transforming her into a vampire, something that Jacob cannot possibly offer.

Ironically, Edward himself cannot see Bella's transformation in the same light. His love for Bella and his belief that he is eternally damned – destined to be cast out of heaven like the soulless monster he believes himself to be – are so strong that he is willing to do whatever he can to ensure her safety and allow her to live a long and healthy human life. While Team Jacob fans argue that Edward's disappearance in *New Moon* was heartless, leaving Bella unprotected when she needed him most (with murderous vamp Victoria come to hunt her down), there's no question that he was acting with Bella's best interests at heart. Recognizing she'll never be entirely safe in the company of his volatile brother, he sets about distancing her from the danger the only way he knows how. In truth, the separation proves no less painful for Edward than for Bella. Yet, irrespective of his own feelings, Edward would rather see Bella forget him, fall for a mortal man like Jacob and live out her natural life with him. Thus the incident with Jasper at the Cullens' house demonstrates just how profound their relationship is – with Edward willing to sacrifice his own happiness for Bella's security, and a future of which Edward himself is no part.

Team Jacob fans see Edward as a self-absorbed narcissist who bullies Bella and doesn't allow her to lead a normal life. Yet this argument ignores a particularly crucial fact of the saga: Bella craves an opportunity to leave the human world to be with Edward, despite the inevitable costs. They also fail to consider that Jacob himself has a violent temper and frequently shows that his loyalty lies with the wolf pack instead of Bella. By contrast, Edward is entirely devoted to Bella, placing his family in danger by forcing them to accept his newfound love despite the threat of exposure she poses to them. Indeed, he values her safety above his own happiness; leaving her behind in order to keep her safe from harm. Jacob, on the other hand, frequently chooses the needs of the pack and his tribe over Bella's needs in times of desperation. While Team Jacob fans argue that cold-blooded beings do not provide the warmth and security of a furry, loving wolf, perhaps they should consider the words of Taylor Lautner regarding his appreciation for the Cullen coven. 'I definitely think it's a prejudice the werewolves have towards all vampires,' said Taylor. 'And especially for

Previous page: *A new brand of rebel: Rob wears his influences on both sleeves for a* New Moon *photo-call in Los Angeles, posing in a leather jacket.*

Opposite: *Rob turns on the red-carpet glamour for the* Vanity Fair *Oscar Party in West Hollywood, March 2009.*

Above left: *Boys will be boys – Rob and his old friend Tom Sturridge enjoy a night out at Los Angeles' Chateau Marmont, November 2008.*

Above right: *And the crowd goes wild! Screaming fans await as Rob leaves the studios of* The Late Show with David Letterman *in New York, November 2009.*

Above: *The* Twilight *trinity – Kristen Stewart, Taylor Lautner, and Robert Pattinson – wave to fans after a photo-call for* New Moon *at Hotel Crillon in Paris, November 2009.*

Opposite: *Are they or aren't they? Rob and Kristen give nothing away at* The Twilight Saga: New Moon *fan event held in Madrid, Spain in November 2009.*

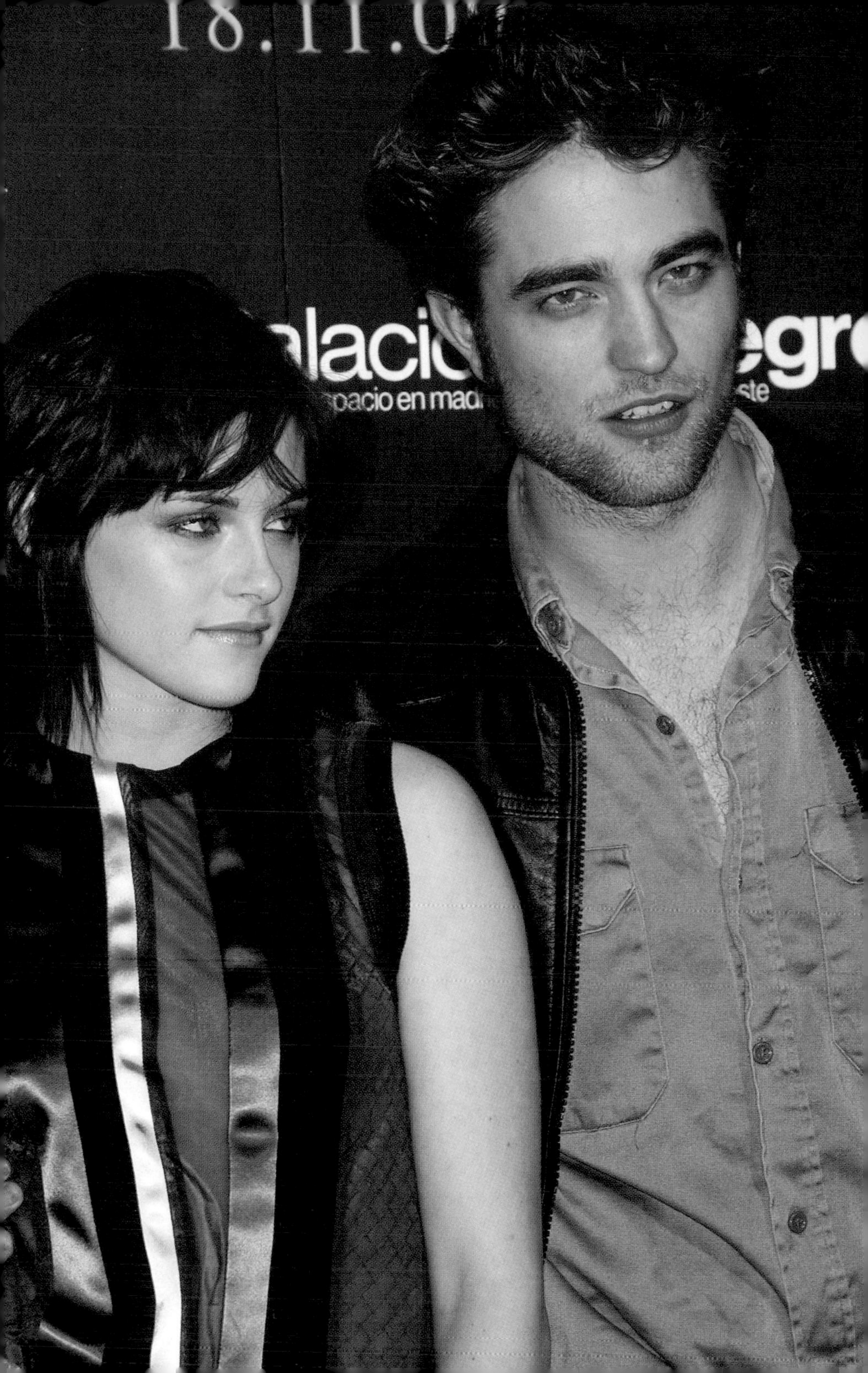

18.11.0
alacio
egr
spacio en madı
ste

Above left: *'Do' the evolution: Rob has another great hair day in November 2009 at* The Twilight Saga: New Moon *fan party at Battersea Evolution, London.*

Above right: *Robert on the Budapest set of* Bel Ami, *March 2010. The film is an adaptation of the 1885 Guy de Maupassant novel, in which Pattinson plays Georges Duroy, an ambitious and immoral journalist.*

Opposite: *Robert as Tyler Hawkins in 2010 romantic drama* Remember Me – *a box-office disappointment better known for its controversial ending than Pattinson's performance.*

Overleaf: *Thanks for the memories: Robert attends a photo-call for* Remember Me *in New York, the city where the film was shot, February 2010.*

Jacob, it's because of Edward Cullen, the guy who has his girl. But, I gotta admit, [the Cullens] are pretty decent vampires.'

Edward is arguably a better protector than Jacob. Though Edward's desire to ensure her safety and happiness is entirely selfless, Jacob Black reveals a side that's quite the opposite – as when he threatens to commit suicide in order to manipulate Bella into kissing him in *Eclipse*. He also enacts petty retribution against Bella by intentionally parking her motorcycle in the driveway where her father Charlie can see it – earning Bella a particularly harsh punishment at the end of *New Moon* (indeed, Miss Swan remains grounded well into the next sequel). Edward's love, on the other hand, is not selfish; he goes so far as to separate himself from Bella just to ensure her survival. In *Eclipse*, he even admits that the best option for Bella would be if she forgot him and moved on with her life, something they both realize she is incapable of doing.

Still, the argument cannot be settled by Taylor Lautner or Robert Pattinson, Team Jacob or Team Edward, or the characters of Jacob and Edward themselves. The choice must be made by Bella. Weighing up her potential love for Jacob, she recognizes that her desire for him is only a fraction of the love that she feels for her bloodsucking beau. The very idea that Bella could live her life without the passion of true love seems even more tragic than her own death. According to Stephenie Meyer, Bella's decision to stay with Edward is rooted in her reluctance to 'settle' for anything less than the eternal love and passion she so greatly desires. Bella understands that Edward has been waiting for her, his soul mate, for more than a century. It is a revelation but also a simple truth, one to which members of Team Jacob remain blind: Bella will never find any human relationship offering anything remotely close to the fairytale she lives with Edward.

No matter how close any other suitor might come in her lifetime, it is clear from Bella's inability to love Jacob on the same level that Edward Cullen is truly her soul mate. An intensely beautiful man, Edward is also in possession of an air of mystery and an edge of danger that many girls find irresistible. But this bad boy has a very soft spot in his heart for his true love. He's proven an undying devotion to her time and time again, making him the safest and ultimately best choice. Certainly, there is no right or wrong answer, though perhaps the final word on the matter should go to the actor who portrays Bella's immortal love. When asked whom he would want his sister to date given the choice between Edward and Jacob, Robert Pattinson thought for a brief moment, chuckled to himself, and in support of his character answered simply: 'Edward's wealthier.'

13
Star-Crossed Crossroads

'Conflict is innate in a lucky person.'
– Robert Pattinson

At twenty-four years old, Robert Pattinson has established himself as one of the biggest and most successful draws in recent box-office history. Thanks to an army of dedicated Team Edward fans, today's production houses know that Rob can fill a theater with starry-eyed teens and grown women enamored of his handsome features and disarming charm. Though Robert has been blessed with the opportunity to play one of the most popular characters in recent film history, the role of Edward Cullen now acts as a proverbial double-edged sword as he pursues new roles and seeks independence from the franchise. As Rob attains the status of Hollywood leading man in years to come, there will be a clear divide among his fans: some will frequent his new films as devotees of Robert Pattinson, the magnetic Barnes-born thespian. Other viewers will see only Edward Cullen's haunting face projected on the big screen.

Robert's first test with audiences as a leading man outside of *Twilight* came on 12 March 2010, with the release of the highly anticipated – yet highly controversial – romantic drama *Remember Me*. Although he had played the lead in smaller indie films, none had inspired such levels of expectation – with studio, press and fans all eagerly awaiting his latest effort. Given his immense success and star power at the time of the film's release, Robert admitted that it was certainly an ongoing challenge for a young man in his position to remain grounded. 'Yes, because the effect of all of this is more terrifying,' he said. 'Success is a thing in which I literally fall into. Probably, if I had worked hard to achieve it, I would see things in a different way, but since I didn't do anything, I am, how can I say, perpetually surprised.'

Announced by Summit Entertainment in 2009, *Remember Me* was billed by the production house's CEO Patrick Wachsberger as 'this generation's *Love Story*'. But thanks to his performance in *Twilight*, Robert Pattinson almost missed out on the starring role. Director Allen Coulter still feels that Pattinson's part as the virtuous vampire failed to exhibit the young actor's range and thespian skills. Fortunately for Robert, Coulter was yet to watch the teen vampire film. 'If I had seen *Twilight* [before casting], I might not have hired him,' he explained. 'He is so limited by the kinds of traits he has to express. It's not that psychologically complex.' Nonetheless, the director was pleased to have taken a chance, saying that despite the limited nature of Edward Cullen's character, he was hopeful that this new role would exhibit the depth of Robert's talent, while the actor's popularity among audiences would certainly fill seats. 'He shows a playful side [in the film],' said Coulter. 'I hope the rabid interest in Rob as a personality helps the box office. It would be foolish to say otherwise.'

Even without Robert, the producers of *Remember Me* had gathered an extremely prestigious cast, reminiscent of the all-star ensemble the Londoner worked with on *Harry Potter and the Goblet of Fire*. His romantic interest Ally is portrayed by the strikingly beautiful and talented Australian actress Emilie de Ravin, best known for her role as Claire in the critically acclaimed television show *Lost*. Pierce Brosnan, who has played sex-symbol special agent James Bond and amassed numerous awards over the past few decades, portrays Pattinson's father, while Academy-Award-nominee Lena Olin (*Chocolat*) plays his mother Diane Hirsch. The supporting roles are rounded out by Oscar- and Golden-Globe-winner Chris Cooper, who plays De Ravin's father, one of the primary sources of tension between the couple. The film was helmed by Allen Coulter, best known for his film *Hollywoodland*. (Released in 2006, *Hollywoodland* was a docudrama that centered on the mysterious death of actor George Reeves and starred Adrien Brody, Diane Lane and Ben Affleck.)

'We've got a really talented cast. Pierce [Brosnan] is playing Rob's dad,' said De Ravin. 'I've got Chris Cooper playing my father. Lena Olin is amazing and we've got a wonderful little eleven-year-old girl, Ruby, who's playing Rob's sister, who's just a sweetheart and really talented. Everyone sort of ended up working together really well too, which is, you know, difficult – especially when you're dealing with family units.'

Remember Me revolves around a pair of young lovers both coping with their own individual family tragedies. Set in the summer of 2001, the story begins with Tyler (Pattinson) trying to break up a street fight. When confronted by the police, Tyler's self-righteousness drives him to hit an officer (Cooper), leading to his arrest and a bloodied face. The arrest acts as a metaphor for Tyler's life, as he clearly needs to be bailed out of his own troubled mindset and difficult circumstances. When Tyler's father

Charles, played by Pierce Brosnan, comes to bail him out, the strain of their relationship is palpable. This turns out to be the result of the suicide of Tyler's brother and his parents' subsequent separation. While attending NYU, Taylor soon meets a young woman named Ally (De Ravin), who is attempting to overcome her own grief after her mother was murdered in front of her when she was a child. Tyler's roommate Aidan recognizes that Ally is the abusive cop's daughter, and persuades Tyler to date and then dump her as retribution against her father. Instead of breaking her heart, Tyler falls in love with her, which only drives a further wedge between Ally and her father.

The love story ends tragically. On a bright Tuesday morning with temperate skies, Tyler goes to the World Trade Center, where his father works, and receives a message that his father is going to be late for their meeting. As he takes the elevator to the ninety-second floor to wait, the date is revealed as 11 September 2001. Tyler is killed when a hijacked plane strikes the tower in that morning's terrorist attacks.

'The premise for the movie is really a romantic tragedy,' De Ravin said. 'My character and Rob's character have both dealt with tragedy in our family and our past and we sort of meet unexpectedly, fall in love unexpectedly and then sort of the way the circumstances that we meet basically threaten to tear us apart. It's really about just treasuring and appreciating every moment you have with loved ones and family because you can never go back.'

Although fate becomes a larger theme as the narrative unfolds, the use of the 9/11 attacks, which was labeled a 'surprise ending' by some media outlets, significantly undermined the film. The movie grossed a meager $8.3 million during its opening weekend in the United States. Worse still, many critics panned *Remember Me* on the basis of what they condemned as an overly tawdry script, with accusations that both director and writer were exploiting the September 11 tragedy in order to compensate for the screenplay's poor quality. (This accusation was perhaps unfair, as an earlier draft of the screenplay shows that the manner of Tyler's death is an integral part of the storyline. In the original version, Tyler's brother has not committed suicide, but was actually killed in the 1993 World Trade Center attacks, eight years prior to the movie's plotline – thus laying the groundwork for the film's controversial ending.)

On account of the tragic twist, Lisa Schwarzbaum of *Entertainment Weekly* rated the film a D+, calling it a 'shameless contraption of ridiculously sad things befalling attractive people'. *Boston Globe* critic Wesley Morris buried the film, rating it a half star out of four. Of the 9/11 issue, Morris wrote that 'the movie crassly repurposes tragedy to excuse its clichés'.

Others focused strictly on the script itself. A.O. Scott of *At the Movies* warned, 'If this movie is playing at a theater near you, you might want to consider moving somewhere else.'

Meanwhile, Manohla Dargis of the *New York Times* wrote: 'In *Remember Me* love means never having to say you're sorry, particularly to the audience.'

But despite the outright contempt frequently directed at the film itself, Robert received a wealth of positive reviews for his efforts. Dargis, though she slated the film in her column, highlighted some of Robert's lighter, transitional scenes, complimenting his performance. 'Mr Pattinson shoots Mr Brosnan a lot of dark, hurting looks,' Dargis wrote, 'but does his best work with Ruby Jerins, an appealing child actress who plays his sister, Caroline. When they're together, Mr Pattinson actually seems happy to be on screen: better yet, he doesn't pull a James Dean Lite, he delivers.' Jake Coyle of the *Associated Press* followed the same formula, bashing the film but praising Rob's performance, writing: 'The most pleasing thing about [the film] is its boldness. It may be affected, but [it] is at least aiming for an intriguing character study – a positive sign in the young career of Pattinson, an actor who was ready to leave behind *Twilight*, apparently in search of his *Five Easy Pieces* or *Rebel Without a Cause*.'

Nonetheless, Robert's personal success remains overshadowed by the controversy surrounding the film's ending. For Americans, 9/11 is one of the most horrific days in living memory and this century's most shockingly callous tragedy. Robert Dougherty, an arts and entertainment critic for *Associated Content*, labeled *Remember Me* the 'most offensive film of the year' in reaction to its final few minutes. The critical consensus is that the film's ending comes out of nowhere. Provided with precious few hints throughout, the audience is given little reason to suspect that the storyline is actually taking place in 2001 and not the present day. But Robert appeared content with the tragic ending, stating that the moment that he finished the script he felt the grief and emotion of that morning in Manhattan, and that the film would not have delivered such a powerful message had it ended any other way. 'When I first read the script, it seemed so much a part of it,' said Robert. 'As soon as I read it, I felt immediately connected to it. If it was edited down in any way, I don't think it would be the same thing. I always feel there's some kind of power to the script. I wanted to keep that in the movie.'

His co-star De Ravin agreed that, although it may come as a shock, the historical relevance resonated powerfully with both the cast and audiences alike. 'For me, it was handled so beautifully,' said De Ravin, 'but it was also just such a surprise to me the first time I read it. I think I've cried every time I've read this script and seen this film – so I might have to walk out when we're watching it! But it's such an important part of history and I think everyone's going to have a completely different opinion because everyone has a different experience, whether they were involved or know somebody involved. Everyone remembers exactly where they were when they heard about it.'

The film itself required a familiar emotional range from Pattinson, as the depressed, unruly character of Tyler shares many of the same qualities as his loner musician Art in *How to Be*. Furthermore, Robert recognized more than a little of his own experience in the conflicted personal life of his character. Tyler is a reclusive young man who has retreated into himself, and has to choose between remaining that way or stepping out into the world to embrace love and life. 'Tyler is so aware of his actions. But he has no idea whether they're of any value at all,' said Robert. 'Can you be a person if you live in the bubble? He's stuck in the middle. At the same time, he's lucky to have the choice. Conflict is innate in a lucky person.' Robert admits that Tyler's issues attracted him to the role. 'I'm a lucky person. Thank God,' Robert said. 'And I'm conflicted. Thank God.'

Remember Me was filmed in New York City in the second half of 2009. Given the shoot's proximity to the release of *New Moon*, Edward-mania was bound to follow Robert to his newest production. As it was being filmed on the campus of New York University (NYU), *Twilight* and Pattinson fans routinely swarmed the set in the hope of catching a glimpse of the handsome young actor. 'We put up barricades ninety feet from the scene, and the people and paparazzi just didn't care,' said Chris Cooper, who won the Oscar for Best Supporting Actor for his role in 2002's *Adaptation*. 'Robert was really under the gun, under a lot of pressure, and I know he's kind of learning to deal with it. And it's a lot to deal with.'

Even for Pierce Brosnan, a Hollywood veteran, the experience of working in front of mobs of people was unlike anything he'd ever known. Having played the iconic role of spy James Bond, Brosnan is no stranger to screaming crowds and blockbuster premieres. But for all his decades in the industry, nothing could have prepared him for the sheer excitement and speculation surrounding Robert and the film's production. 'I've never encountered such attention in my career,' said Brosnan. 'I mean, I certainly had [this level of popularity] but on a day-to-day basis, this young man certainly acquitted himself very well. And I think he was just completely blindsided by everything. And here he was doing a drama, which he's executive producer on, and he had a heavy workload every day, and it's a hard one to be wrenched out of every time you step out of your trailer.'

The hype surrounding *Twilight* and *New Moon* had followed Robert, with each and every detail of his on-set movements popping up on blogs and news sites at all hours of the day and night. 'There's nowhere to hide. There's nowhere to run,' said Brosnan. 'You know, you're damned if you do, and you're damned if you don't . . . You have to go to emotional places where you really need to [put your] head down and [look] straight ahead.' But even when he put his head down, fans and photographers were still snapping pictures and speculating about Robert's activities, sparking rumors that he had been injured on set. A number of paparazzi shots of Robert wearing make-up that made him appear bloody and cut popped up on websites around the world. Headlines accompanying the pictures included 'Pattinson's Bloody Monday'. Several independent sources implied that Robert had been hurt while filming, or worse, gotten into a tussle while taking time away from the set. However, these concerns were easily dismissed as random conjecture when it was revealed that his 'wounds' were just make-up and central to the film's opening sequences, in which he is arrested by his love interest's father.

Chris Cooper, who plays Ally's father, blamed 'instant messaging' for the swarms of people who would arrive daily to watch production of the outdoor shots. ('Instant messaging' is Cooper's blanket term for text messaging, Facebook, MySpace and Twitter.) Given that filming took place at NYU, the presence of so many young female fans – all of who turned out in the hope of catching a glimpse of Robert – seems natural enough. 'He was doing scenes with a crowd of people thirty feet away from him and the paparazzi would not stop clicking the camera and there was a couple of hot, heated periods with the director [Allen Coulter] with that kind of intrusion,' Chris said. 'I know at his age, no way I could have handled it.'

Brosnan recognized that while he was still an immensely popular actor, his effect on women could not compete with the *Twilight* star's. 'I have no remaining ego whatsoever after shooting *Remember Me* with Robert,' says Brosnan. 'His trailer was down one end of the avenue, surrounded by girls, and mine was a very quiet little haven of solitude at the other end.'

De Ravin commented on the complications of working with an ever-present audience, telling of how it grew increasingly difficult to focus on her work with the curious crowds congregating outside the set's barriers. 'Um, yeah, you know, it took a little getting used to,' the actress said. 'We really shot the majority of the film on location, you know, in and around Manhattan so there's just people everywhere anyway. It got a little hectic at times! The first day I was sort of like, "Oh my God. How am I going to focus?" And you know, there were times that we were rehearsing and you can't even sort of think about what you're doing. You feel all these eyes on you and you become very suddenly self-conscious about what's going on as opposed to being in your own little world of the character.'

Although the film failed to generate a blockbuster opening weekend, Robert had firmly established himself among an all-star cast who recognized his talent and charm. '[Robert's] such a nice, genuine, great guy as a person,' said De Ravin. 'And you know that's always nice when you're working with someone you get along with. [He's] very giving. We sort of worked on stuff a lot together and we'd talk about things and really developed our characters together as much as we could. And that's a real give and take thing if you've got one person not wanting to do that and one that does – it sort of creates a bit of conflict. But we were both sort of on the same page with everything, which was great.'

Despite the critical uproar provoked by its controversial ending, Robert defended the film and his decision to star in it. *Remember Me* signals his undying commitment to character-driven pieces, enabling him to cultivate his craft and explore the full range of his acting abilities. With *Eclipse*, the third installment in the *Twilight* series, fast approaching, Robert has already signed on for a number of other films in 2010 and beyond that will truly test him as an actor. Given his immense popularity, however, the biggest challenge of all for Rob remains personal – that of striking a delicate balance between his everyday existence and his glittering new public persona as one of the most popular actors in Hollywood today.

14
today's Actor, tomorrow's Rock Star

'I used to play music all the time, and the most amazing part was the freedom that
came with kicking myself in the ass, letting go, and surprising myself.'
– Robert Pattinson

Whether Robert Pattinson will eventually cross over into the music business is a question burning in the minds of many of the actor's most devoted fans. Following his successful contribution to the *Twilight* soundtrack (Rob's haunting vocals can be heard on two of the movie's best-loved songs), it seems a natural progression for the gifted young star – as it has been for many actors before him, including Jamie Foxx and Robert Downey Jr. Speculation in early 2010 even tied Robert to British mogul Simon Cowell, though it was later revealed that no such deal had been offered to Pattinson. (A source close to the speculation told the *Sun*: 'Robert was reluctant to be turned into a pop star – he takes his music very seriously. He is a bit wary of signing up with Cowell, who is, of course, associated with *X Factor* and pop.')

To *Twilight* fans' delight, Rob has been writing his own music for quite some time, drawing inspiration from a number of his favorite artists. Describing his material as 'Van Morrison-ish, Jeff Buckley-ish stuff', he has no plans to release an album in the immediate future, saying that he doesn't want to venture into his sister's line of work for fear of being branded a 'franchise'. 'It is always kind of embarrassing when actors are playing music,' Robert said, 'and it's very frustrating, I don't know why there's such a stigma attached to it. You always come across as being like a franchise person who's going to then release a fragrance and a clothing line.'

Yet it's not something he's ready to rule out altogether. Recording an album is a longstanding ambition of Robert's and it seems he'll stop at nothing to make it happen on his own terms – even if this means adopting a cryptic pseudonym. 'I might make an album,' he said, 'but not through a record company or anything. I'd like to do something independent. I'd just like to have it just for myself so I can work with good musicians and stuff.' He later added, 'Maybe I could just do it under "Edward Cullen" and see what happens.'

Still, Robert remains an avid amateur musician and fan of multiple genres, having played the piano since the age of three. As he grew older, he learned the guitar and sought additional influences and styles to incorporate into his own. 'I have been playing the piano for my entire life – since I was three or four,' he said. 'And the guitar – I used to play classical guitar from when I was about five to twelve years of age. Then I didn't play guitar for years. About four or five years ago, I got out the guitar again and just started playing blues and stuff. I am not very good at the guitar, but I am alright.'

Robert's involvement with the guitar eventually led him to form the band Bad Girls. Describing its origins, he said, 'Bad Girls belonged to my first girlfriend's current boyfriend and he was having an open-mic night. He invited me to sing, but it was just a bit of fun. We only played a couple of gigs. It is just a couple of friends of mine and some other people that I had met fairly recently. We just wanted to start a band for something to do. A lot of my friends are actors and we have so little to do all the time, so instead of just being bored, we were like, "Why not start a band?" So we did. I had kind of roll-on, roll-off musicians. I still try and play, but it's weird now since when I'm trying to do it as an actor, it always seems kind of cheesy. I liked playing at open mics in bars and stuff because it was the only time I really felt free. I did a couple of gigs in LA and people filmed [them] and put them on the internet. It just ruins the whole experience. You're like, "Oh, that wasn't the point." So I stopped. I'm going to wait for all this to die down before I start doing live gigs again.'

Robert's fondness for music also provided him with a much-needed creative outlet while his indie film career was making slow progress in 2006. 'I think you need to be able to break through what you think about yourself to try to make any sort of art,' Robert said. 'I used to play music all the time, and the most amazing part was the freedom that came with kicking myself in the ass, letting go, and surprising myself.' While living in Soho, prior to the *Twilight* hype, he joined up with a gang of musicians known as the 'Brit Pack', taking part in Up All Night open-mic events. The four musicians who comprised the Brit Pack were Robert, Bobby Long, Sam Bradley and Marcus Foster. Foster and Bradley have known Pattinson since their time at Harrodian. Bobby Long met the crew through Up All Night founder Phil Taylor. Having all worked in collaboration with Pattinson in some manner, each exerted an individual influence that later impacted upon Pattinson's style. According to Robert, Bradley leans towards a rock vibe, Long is more folksy, and Foster exhibits shades of veteran singer-songwriter Tom Waits when performing. 'I grew up with some amazing musicians in London who are still my friends,' said Robert. 'Marcus Foster, Bobby Long and Sam Bradley are recording their albums now, but Johnny Flynn [a British folk-rock singer-songwriter] completed his one a while ago. I just saw him play in LA and he was incredible. But he's always been incredible so I can't say I was surprised. The album is great; no one else does music like him at all.'

Van Morrison stands out as one of Robert's strongest musical influences, and Pattinson claims that two songs by the musician, 'Stepping Out Queen, Pt. II' and 'T.B. Sheets', are fixtures in his portable music players. '[Van Morrison is] another guy who has such a visionary and unique take on what structure in songwriting is, what singing is, and what can be achieved emotionally and spiritually through music,' Robert said.

Morrison, best known for his timeless song 'Brown Eyed Girl', is so central to Pattinson's music and creative life that the young actor has said that he'd love to portray him in a film one day. Although there is no script currently in development about the famous songwriter, this hasn't stopped Rob from speculating. 'I'd love to play Van Morrison, but I doubt I would get the part,' he said. Other musical favorites of Robert's include the Black Keys, Tom Waits, Kings of Leon, James Brown, and Neil Young.

The *Twilight* soundtrack provided Robert's first and only experience of producing music for mass distribution. It featured two of his songs in addition to a number of tracks by Muse, Linkin Park and Paramore, among others. But even amidst these big-name acts, Robert's songs 'Never Think' and 'Let Me Sign' stand out as the two most critical pieces of his fledgling music career.

'I did them before the movie. But it's amazing how they fit,' Robert said. 'Like I would never have said, I really want to get my songs in the movie. I thought it was kind of funny. There's a song which two friends of mine wrote in about three minutes and I sang it in my old apartment. I kind of made it into a song and now it's in this big movie. I thought it was kind of amusing. I had to sing it to the video of my face. It was the most bizarre experience, but I think it really helps the scene. It makes the scene better.'

'I asked Robert if he was interested in writing the love theme and he went, "Not really. No, that's not my thing,"' said Catherine Hardwicke. 'I mean, he's not like an artist that you give an assignment to and he completes the assignment. For Rob, it flows out of him. He's more of an organic artist. When he feels something that's when he creates. You can't tell him, "Do this. Do a love theme for Bella that will be used throughout the movie and translates to six different instruments." That's not the way he creates. So, he never wrote a love theme for Bella.

'What he did the day we shot the piano for the first time was he sat down and improvised for the hour we filmed,' Hardwicke later said. 'He improvised beautifully. I mean, he's such a musician. Just beautiful things and melodies, but it wasn't an intentional theme that could be used in different parts of the movie and developed and orchestrated with the violins and everything. He just let it flow. So the composer, Carter Burwell, did compose this beautiful love theme and that is developed in the early stages, in biology class, and then it keeps growing and goes through different instrumentations, and finally recorded with a full orchestra. When we re-shot the scene, Rob played that love theme on the piano.'

Robert initially had no plans to be part of the soundtrack, but his popularity would drive fans' curiosity about his ability to play, write and perform. While this certainly helped sell millions of copies, adding fuel to the hype surrounding Robert's hidden talents, looking back it appears that the experience was never something that he was comfortable with.

'I didn't really think about it beforehand,' Robert said. 'I didn't know it was going to be on the soundtrack or anything. I wanted to do it under another name because I thought it would be distracting, which it has been. So it's probably all been a big mistake, but I like the idea of it and I just think the song fits and I did not think it sounded like me. So I thought it would just work, but I don't know. I'm not trying to get a music career out of it or anything.'

Robert Pattinson's increasing fame has naturally created interest in all aspects of his life. From his taste in music to his taste in women, speculation about his daily existence has reached the cover of every online blog and magazine and – adorned with Rob's chiseled features and deep, blue eyes – they sell. Unsurprisingly, news of Robert's love life has been most coveted of all. Over the years, Hollywood tabloids have linked Pattinson with several of the most glamorous women in the public eye, including Brazilian model Annelyse Schoenberger. Yet, gossip mills want nothing more than confirmation that Robert Pattinson and Kristen Stewart are together and living out Edward and Bella's love in reality.

Pattinson's interest in his co-star has at times seemed mutual, as Stewart compliments Robert on a near-constant basis. In one interview she gushed, 'Oh, he's like a little tortured artist. He's British. He's tall. He always looks like he's thinking about something. And he's quite witty. So he's pretty sexy.'

The speculation surrounding the two has reached such a level of absurdity that even British officials are taking an interest in the couple, fueling rumors of an off-screen romance. In February 2010, Nicolas Clark spotted Pattinson and Stewart hidden away in a cozy corner of a London pub. The politician hastily posted on his Twitter account, 'In The Marquis of Granby with Robert Pattinson & Kristen Stewart.' A few hours later he added: 'From what I saw just a couple of kisses on lips,' and then, 'R+K were acting like a couple.' Yet, for all the hearsay surrounding the *Twilight* lovers, a picture is worth a thousand words. And New Year's 2009 yielded some of the most intriguing images of the young stars yet.

'I still haven't found one place in the world where I could disappear,' Rob once claimed, telling *Première* magazine: 'Even in the most remote location you could imagine, there'd be someone asking me to be in a picture.' Months later, he put his theory to the test – leaving the paparazzi dazed, confused and hunting for headlines elsewhere. Contrary to everything you'd expect of Hollywood's hottest young couple, Rob and Kristen opted to see in 2010 in a secret location on the Isle of Wight. Set just off the south coast of England, this island is not the most 'remote' destination you could imagine, but, with its chalky-white cliffs and vivid green landscapes, it's certainly one of the most beautiful. A true-life version of Edward and Bella's meadow, it was the perfect place for the two young stars to hide themselves from the prying eyes of the media, whose attentions, according to Kristen, can only 'debase' the special bond she's formed with her *Twilight* co-star.

However, while Rob and Kristen will go to any lengths to escape a paparazzo's lens, it seems they'll always have time for genuine fans of *The Twilight Saga*. Clad in low-key hoodies, the actors were more than happy to pose for pictures with the disbelieving young Twilighter who spotted them – surreally enough – on a walk along Ventnor high street on New Year's Eve. Predictably, the tabloids seized on this unexpected sighting of 'Robsten', immediately reporting: '*Twilight* stars look for love nest on the Isle of Wight'. While such headlines seem premature to say the least, the shy hint of a smile on Rob's lips left many Twi-hards wondering if they'd get their wish for true-life romance after all . . .

Or would they? Months later, a question mark still hangs over the true nature of Rob's relationship with Kristen, with neither tight-lipped actor liable to put an end to the speculation any time soon. 'I probably would've answered [. . .] if people hadn't made such a big deal about it,' sighed Kristen in interview with *Entertainment Weekly*, 'but I'm not going to give the fiending an answer!' With conflicting reports appearing every other day, 'Robsten' remains as maddening a mystery as ever, even in the aftermath of 2010's BAFTA Awards.

Both Rob and Kristen turned out for the glittering ceremony, held in London's Royal Opera House on 21 February. And, though the two young stars arrived separately, maintaining a careful distance on the red carpet, no one failed to notice them leaving together. Climbing into the same car as Anna Kendrick (who plays Bella's friend Jessica in *The Twilight Saga*), the young couple headed for the after-party with true cause for celebration.

Still glowing from Kristen's win (she'd just been named Orange Rising Star), and rocking a suave new hairstyle to match his designer suit, the elusive Mr Pattinson reportedly had words with a *Sun* journalist that night, and the tabloid newspaper subsequently published what they claimed was the first public confirmation of the budding romance.

Splashed across next morning's edition, the British paper announced that 'R-Patz admits: I AM With K-Stew'. Rob allegedly confided, 'It is extremely difficult but we are together, yes,' insisting that all the couple's 'cloak-and-dagger' tactics were called for, if only to minimize the impact of Robsten's first appearance as a couple. 'We can't arrive at the same time because of the fans,' he is said to have explained (and indeed, Kristen did arrive on the night flanked by six bodyguards). 'It goes crazy. This was supposed to be a public appearance as a couple but it's impossible. We are here together and it's a public event but it's not easy. We have to do all this stuff to avoid attention.'

Whether such reports are to be believed or not; whatever happens between Rob and Kristen when the cameras stop rolling, the *Twilight* franchise has made this young couple wealthy beyond their wildest dreams. Robert Pattinson was named as the thirty-fifth wealthiest celebrity of 2009 with a fortune of $18 million. Kristen herself was valued at nearly $16 million. The idea that media attention alone should prevent Robert from living the life he chooses, with whomsoever he chooses, should hopefully be disproved with time.

Indeed, for true fans of Team Edward, the most important rumors center on Robert Pattinson's upcoming roles and the potential scripts that he is reading. While he recently moved forward with his post-*Twilight* career with his performance in *Remember Me*, the years 2010 and 2011 will undoubtedly ensure that gossip magazines adorned with pictures of his face continue to fly off the shelves, as the young actor has a full slate of roles that should set him up as a future leading star and potential Oscar contender.

15

the Year of Robert Pattinson

'I know it will take me at least another ten years before I'm remotely satisfied with anything I do. But with acting you keep trying in the hopes you might be great.'
– Robert Pattinson

Eclipse is anticipated to be one of the highest-grossing films of 2010, carrying on the now-established tradition of *Twilight* mania leading up to an overcharged premiere and a record-breaking weekend to follow. But Robert has his sights set on much more this year than acclaim for his second reprisal of the role of Edward Cullen. Pattinson has a full slate of films currently in some level of production that will allow him to branch out and pursue new roles with some of Hollywood's best and brightest stars, including several Academy-Award-winning and nominated actors and actresses. As was the case with his lengthy search for dark, indie roles several years earlier, Robert spent a great deal of time perusing scripts and researching time periods for the perfect match. Just as he chose to portray Art in *How to Be* or Tyler in *Remember Me*, Robert is now trying to select roles that are applicable to his present mood or the current state of his life. 'I try to choose things which are something that I'm going through in my life,' he said. 'Jobs that will help me realize or add something about myself. I don't really think about it in terms of a career.'

So far it looks as though Pattinson will remain busy for 2010 and part of 2011, his schedule stocked with parts that offer him a very broad range of characters to research and develop. 'I judge things purely on the script. I'm booked up for this year. I've been doing the most different things you can possibly imagine. Every part is so different. I can't say any of the parts I'm doing – they haven't been finalized yet. But I don't pick them in terms of genre; purely the script. If I like the script and I like the part, then that's all that matters.'

Robert's first test following the release of *Eclipse* will be a supporting role in the directorial debut of Madeleine Stowe – the American western *Unbound Captives*. Starring Hugh Jackman, the film is about a frontiersman, Tom (Jackman), who helps a young woman named May (Rachel Weisz) find her children after they are kidnapped and her husband is killed by a Comanche war party in 1859. Tom and May venture out to try to find the children, and over the years their relationship eventually becomes romantic. (It's worth noting that although this movie is set in the Old West, the lead actor and actress are from Australia and England respectively.)

Unbound Captives is the writing and directorial debut of the multi-talented Madeleine Stowe, best known for her riveting performance in the 1996 psychological thriller *Twelve Monkeys*. Fox Studios had initially offered Stowe and her co-writer and husband Brian Benben $3 million, and later $5 million, for the original script, a remarkable amount of money for anyone selling their first story. The studio reportedly planned to develop the movie with Ridley Scott as director and Russell Crowe as its star. However, Stowe turned down the offer because there was no promise she would be anything more than the screenwriter.

In the film, Robert plays one of the kidnapped children who has grown up and does not remember his mother when she finally does locate him and his sister. 'I'm playing a kid who was kidnapped by the Comanche when he was four years old and he's brought up by them. Then his mother spends her entire life trying to find me and my sister. When she finds us we can't remember who she is and can't remember anything about the western culture that she grew up in. I speak Comanche in the whole movie.' Robert added, 'You can't really speak more differently from Edward,' suggesting that he was eager to temporarily step away from the role that had brought him international acclaim.

Robert was eager to learn the Comanche language for the role, but said that the script intrigued him mostly because it reminded him of one of his favorite movies, *Giant*. 'I actually signed on to that after I had done *Twilight*, in the summer, just a couple of months after I finished. It was really before anything had happened, so I wasn't really thinking about it. It was just a cool script and it reminded me, in a lot of ways, of *Giant*, which is one of my favorite movies. I think that's why I responded to it.'

Robert's next historical film in 2010 will be the Depression-era drama *Water for Elephants*, which centers on a Cornell veterinary student who drops out of university and joins the circus after his parents are killed in a car accident. (At the time of writing, IMDB has announced the film's title as *Circus*, although the script has not been finalized.) Based on Sara Gruen's bestselling novel, the film adaptation will bring Pattinson together with Academy-Award winners Sean Penn and Reese Witherspoon, the latter also starred in his first film *Vanity Fair*.

After losing his parents, Pattinson's character leaves the college town of Ithaca. Joining the Benzini Brothers' Most Spectacular Show on Earth, he finds himself working as a veterinarian for the circus. Witherspoon will play equestrian star Marlena, who is married to August, a twisted animal trainer, played by Penn. The adaptation will be directed by Francis Lawrence, best known for his dark blockbuster *I Am Legend*, with a script penned by Richard LaGravenese, writer of *The Fisher King*, *The Bridges of Madison County* and *The Horse Whisperer*. It is expected that the film will be shot on Cornell University's campus during the summer of 2010 while the majority of the students are away for the summer break.

Robert is also set to play a sexually-charged journalist in the period piece *Bel Ami* – filming in early 2010 and due for release in 2011. Based on the 1885 novel by French author Guy de Maupassant, *Bel Ami* is a moral tale centered on journalist Georges Duroy (Robert Pattinson), who travels through 1890s Paris, using his wits and powers of seduction to rise from poverty to wealth by manipulating a series of powerful mistresses. 'It's a bit of bedroom drama. It's a romance between Rob and a number of Parisian housewives,' said co-star Uma Thurman, best known for her roles in *Pulp Fiction* and the *Kill Bill* volumes. Initially Nicole Kidman had been rumored to take the part of Pattinson's primary love interest Madeleine, but negotiations with the Australian actress never came to anything, and Thurman won the part. The film's story focuses on many of the same vices as *Vanity Fair*, but is far fiercer; depicting a world of political and media corruption, where sex is power and celebrity a valuable commodity. Kristin Scott Thomas (*Nowhere Boy*, *I've Loved You So Long*) stars as Duroy's other love interest Virginie; Christina Ricci (*Monster*, *The Ice Storm*) as Clotilde; and Holly Grainger (*The Scouting Book for Boys*, *The Bad Mother's Handbook*) as Suzanne. Filmed in London and Budapest, the film is being produced by Simon Fuller, founder of *American Idol* and former manager of the Spice Girls.

While these three roles promise to establish the young heartthrob as one of Hollywood's leading men, there is only one forthcoming role that Pattinson's Twi-hard truly fans care about. At the moment, dates for the *Breaking Dawn* shoot remain unconfirmed by Summit Entertainment. The most controversial installment of the *Twilight Saga*, it has been rumored that the studio is hesitant to take it to the big screen. However, if it is made, Summit may decide to split the novel into two distinct films in the same fashion as *Harry Potter and the Deathly Hallows*. Given the immense success of the first two films, and the blockbuster returns expected from *Eclipse*, Summit will most likely target a release date in 2011, working from a carefully edited script that may, or may not, aim to steer around the gorier aspects of the book.

It is expected that Robert Pattinson, Taylor Lautner and Kristen Stewart will demand significant sums for the fourth, and, potentially, fifth films. While Summit are likely to agree to major pay increases for the three young stars who have become synonymous with the success of the franchise, both Stewart and Pattinson have signaled a desire to move beyond the vampire melodrama series as soon as shooting and promotion of all of the films has been completed.

While neither has capitalized on their roles in the series by signing with a major studio, both expect solid returns on their smaller-scale leading roles like Stewart's upcoming 1980s punk-rock biopic *The Runaways* and Pattinson's *Remember Me*, also produced by Summit. Of his mission to find future roles that would distance him from the vampire franchise, Robert told one interviewer, 'Hey, if you hear of one, let me know. Anything that has nothing to do with blood, I hope.'

Still, Robert doesn't appear to be too concerned about the future. 'I'm not massively concerned about doing lots of acting jobs,' he said. 'If it all just went, right now, I'd be like, "All right. I don't really care." That's probably a stupid thing to say. But I don't, really. I think it'd be much worse to do a load of stuff that's really bad. Because then you can't go into another career. If you've made an idiot out of yourself, you're never going to be taken seriously, as a lawyer or something, if you're, like, a joke actor. The only thing I want from anything is to not be embarrassed.'

For Robert Pattinson, the road to stardom has been paved with a series of highlights and setbacks, cinematic franchises with massive premiere crowds and undiscovered indie gems, attended by a faithful few viewers. While Team Jacob's Taylor Lautner is poised to become the next big-budget action star, Rob has shown no more interest in such adrenaline-fueled scripts than before, sticking to his preferred roles in intense, character-driven films. His three period pieces – *Bel Ami*, *Unbound Captives*, and *Water for Elephants* – are reminiscent of the roles taken by elite actors such as Johnny Depp, who made a conscious decision in his early career to think long term. Honing his chosen craft, Depp's focus has been the beautiful and challenging process of creating something unique and lasting with every role he's ever pursued. While this strategy poses a greater challenge for anyone planning to remain in Hollywood for decades – in the manner of Robert's enduring idol, Jack Nicholson –

Pattinson seems content with establishing himself one film at a time, one scene at a time, until he feels comfortable in his skin as a leading man.

What Pattinson's career has shown time and time again is that, at twenty-four years old, he will continue to pursue roles with which he feels personally satisfied, spending his free time and shaping his future however he sees fit – be it playing music in a dimly-lit Soho pub or picking up a script for a low-budget film that doesn't have enough money to house its stars. Whatever inspires him to remain creative all the days of his career, Robert Pattinson will pursue.

With a full slate of highly anticipated films coming up this year and next, Robert appears set for even higher levels of critical acclaim. At the same time, he will remain true to himself, to his craft and to his creative urges, no matter what the size of the budget or the anticipated critical reception. 'Before, I felt like I couldn't break through anything, including myself. And now it feels a bit as though I've climbed along the side of my brain and am at least looking in. But I know it will take me at least another ten years before I'm remotely satisfied with anything I do. But with acting you keep trying in the hopes you might be great. But then I think, does wanting to be good or even great, or even just wanting to make art, cheapen the experience?'

That is for Robert Pattinson alone to decide.